For many years, Warrant Officer North has been both a good friend and a greatly valued contact within the Military Intelligence community. He's lived what techno-thriller authors only write about. You can count of one thing with this most excellent book on the Iraqi conflict: he's giving you the real story.

James Cobb
Author of The Arctic Event and the
Amanda Garret techno-thriller series

Hunting Muqtada

HAROLD M. NORTH

iUniverse, Inc.
New York   Bloomington

iUniverse books may be ordered through booksellers or by contacting:

iUniverse
1663 Liberty Drive
Bloomington, IN 47403
www.iuniverse.com
1-800-Authors (1-800-288-4677)

ISBN: 978-1-4401-2463-1 (pbk)
ISBN: 978-1-4401-2464-8 (ebk)

Printed in the United States of America

Library of Congress Control Number: 2009924013

iUniverse rev. date: 3/4/2009

To Joe, Paul, Sami and Leyla
The True Heroes of This Story
Thanks for Watching my Back

For reasons of Operations Security, and in the interests of the safety of the Military Intelligence professionals depicted in this book that have had contact with members of listed terrorist organizations, and in the interests of the safety of their families, the names of those individuals have been changed.

Terrorists in custody at the Guantanamo Bay holding facility in Cuba have spent many hundreds of hours with U.S. Military Intelligence personnel in interrogations and debriefings. The terrorists have been caught attempting to write to contacts in the Middle East, giving the names of their captors, the names of their other family members and children, and where in the United States they lived. Assassins were to be dispatched to the Soldiers' homes to kill every man, woman and child there.

The threat is real.

If there must be trouble,
Let it be in my day,
So that my children may have peace.

~Thomas Paine

This book was written in diary format day-to-day during the war, from the perspective of a Soldier in the field, reflecting on the events as they happened, as well as the thoughts, feelings and comments of the other Soldiers around me. This not just my story, but theirs as well.

Contents

CHAPTER 1
KUFA AND NAJAF

DAY 146: SUN 5 OCT 03

I was surrounded by history. I had been walking, eating and sleeping on the decaying ruins of the ancient city of Babylon beside the Euphrates River for the past six weeks. The crumbling foundations of the Tower of Babel were only yards from my desk. The wall of King Nebuchadnezzar's throne chamber—whereupon God had written with His finger—was only a stone's throw from my sleeping tent. This same chamber was the last known resting place of Alexander the Great, before his remains had disappeared into the sands of history.

But just as ancient history surrounded me, there was modern history here as well. One of Saddam Hussein's 70-plus gaudy desert-colored palaces stood on a perfectly rounded hilltop overlooking the ruins. Much to the dismay of archeologists, bulldozers had scraped up ruins into the huge pile to form the hill. Countless artifacts that archeologists had never had an opportunity to examine had been destroyed and lost forever so Saddam could have his hill. Looters from the nearby town of Hilla had stripped the palace down to its bare Italian marble walls long before the coalition had arrived. It now resembled a

1

cool, dark cavern wherein one could escape the brutal heat of the day, even without any functioning air conditioning.

Untold further damage was done when Saddam had directed the construction of a convention center and its entire supporting infrastructure at the base of his palace hill. Archeological destruction was multiplied exponentially when Saddam directed the resurrection of the ruins—by literally building on top of the remaining crumbling walls. Babylon was ringed with a number of brick factories that had been commissioned to provide all of the bricks to rebuild the entire city—supposedly as close to the original as was possible—by piling his new bricks on top of the 4,000-year-old originals. Nebuchadnezzar had a limited number of special bricks with his name inscribed on them claiming responsibility for building Babylon. Saddam had some patterned after Nebuchadnezzar's, taking credit for its resurrection that were found in walls randomly throughout the ruins. I wondered if God, annoyed with Saddam for rebuilding Babylon in his own image, was using us to symbolically destroy it once again.

Saddam's goal was to transform Babylon into a worldwide tourist attraction, a vacation resort for the rich and famous. Instead, the area had served as the headquarters of the First Marine Division, United States Marine Corps. The Marines had been here since the end of major hostilities in May 2003 until September, when they rotated back home. Camp Babylon, as it had been christened, was now the headquarters for the newly-formed Multi-National Division, or MND. Led by a brigade from the Polish army, who provided the largest contingency of any other nation, the MND was responsible for security in the five provinces identified as South-Central Iraq.

South-Central Iraq was practically void of U.S. forces. The coalition commander, Lieutenant General Ricardo S. Sanchez, wanted American eyes and ears on the ground to provide him directly with ground-truth intelligence. This was where our little group of Soldiers came in. I was part of a Military Intelligence company of less than 40 Americans, all mobilized reservists. We were spread throughout the five provinces, tasked with tracking not only insurgents, but keeping an eye on our coalition partners as well—not so much to 'spy' on them as to keep General Sanchez apprised of their activities, or lack of them as the case may be.

Our recent experiences in the Balkans had taught us that our coalition partners did not always act in open faith or in the best interests of the coalition. Some partners in Bosnia had been caught running guns, drugs and/or prostitution rings, and were now also represented in our newly formed Iraqi coalition as well. And of course, despite the outward façade of being coalition partners, many of them spied on us as much as—or even more so than—the enemy. One coalition partner had brought along their signal intercept vans and placed them on some hills in the camp. However, instead of facing their collection dishes outwards towards town, they pointed into the camp—towards us.

Our company had already been in Iraq for six months, since the end of major hostilities in May 2003. We had spent those months in a camp northeast of Baghdad screening over 4,000 freedom fighters classified by our illustrious State Department at the insistence of former President Clinton as 'terrorists,' in a failed effort to curry favor with the "evil terrorist mullah regime" of Iran, as these freedom fighters referred to them. With only 12 hours' notice we were ordered to leave the camp and head south to Camp Babylon and conduct our current mission. We had been here six weeks so far.

I was the officer in charge of our company's night shift, as we ran 24-hour operations to support our five teams in the field, one in each province. I had served in the military in various capacities for the last 21 years: as an armor crewman on an M-60 tank in a cavalry troop, as a Special Operations Combat Controller in the Air Force, then back in the Army as an interrogator in Military Intelligence. I had been appointed a warrant officer in the early 1990s, and also had the honor of serving as a competitive member of the U.S. Shooting Team at one point in my career.

Some of our Soldiers had been previously mobilized under Operation Enduring Freedom in support of operations in Afghanistan. They were shortly coming up on their two-year limit of presidential authority for mobilization, and would be going home earlier than the rest of us. This re-deployment would leave us even more short-handed, but we had no choice but to adapt and continue the mission. Our company commander, Captain Oliver, and our Operations Officer, Captain Dave, had notified me the night before that in a couple of weeks or so, I would move to the city of Najaf to replace the current team leader that had to rotate back home soon. This duo had been aptly nicknamed "Captains Courageous" by the members of the company.

Captain Dave caught me in the hall after breakfast. He was tall and lean, with curly black hair and a long, a scruffy face that almost always bore a smile. His demonstrated care and concern for the Soldiers coupled with his easy demeanor and superior diplomatic skills made Dave one of the finest officers I had the pleasure of working for in my 21-year career to date. All of us felt blessed to have him with us during this particularly difficult period in our lives—serving in Iraq for a year, far from home and our families. For many of us, he made it almost bearable.

"Hey, Harry, can you come in here for a bit? Oliver and I need to talk with you." He invited me into the Captain Oliver's office. For reasons of Operations Security, our entire company was on a first-name or nickname basis, even between officers and enlisted. As Military Intelligence Soldiers surrounded by foreign armies—even coalition ones—we wanted to do what we could to maintain our own anonymity. Many members of our unit also had civilian careers with other national intelligence agencies when not mobilized as reservists.

Oliver's office was bare except for two desks, one for him and the other for our First Sergeant. On the wall behind Oliver's desk hung a British Sterling 9-millimeter sub-machine gun with an integral suppressor. It had belonged to a member of Saddam's elite bodyguards at one point. Oliver's solid frame was capped with salt-and-pepper hair that seemed to have become saltier since our deployment. His long nose was framed by bright blue eyes that seemed to have lost a bit of their shine from the burden of command that he carried. He almost always exercised his light sense of humor even in the most trying circumstances. He had been hastily appointed the commander immediately before leaving for Iraq when the previous commander had been accused of sexual harassment by another female Soldier. Dave shut the door and the three of us sat in a triangle of chairs, all facing one another in a small huddle.

Captain Oliver spoke first. "Harry, I know we told you to expect to move to Najaf in the next few weeks, but we need to move up the time table. You're going today."

To say I was stunned would be an understatement. Mentally, I hadn't prepared for such a quick change in scenery and activity. I tried to remain straight-faced, and continued to listen.

"Kinysha will be rotating home early, and you will replace her there as the team leader. That's still the plan. However, the other team members there are having...issues with her. We need you to go back with them today and for now, just observe and learn. Kinysha will brief you on all you need to know to take over before she leaves in the next few weeks."

Dave took over the conversation. "We've learned from the Soldiers on her team that she has been, well, difficult to work with. We're hoping your presence there will help calm the situation some."

It felt like I was being tossed into a room full of powder kegs holding a kerosene-dripping torch in each hand. Dave continued, "We need you to look for anything out of the ordinary, and keep us apprised."

One by one, the teams from each province all rolled into camp in their Japanese-made pickup trucks and SUVs, referred to as Non-Tactical Vehicles (NTVs) in Army-speak. We didn't travel in our unit High Mobility Multi-Purpose Wheeled Vehicles (HMMWVs, commonly called "humvees") because there weren't enough seats for all our Soldiers. We had acquired a small fleet of civilian vehicles confiscated from Saddam's government by the Marines.

The teams exchanged information and briefed everyone on the latest situation in each province. Intelligence reports were sent up to higher headquarters for further analysis and cross-referencing. I hastily packed my equipment and bags, loaded them into the two pickup trucks for Tactical Human Intelligence Team (THT) 108, and we headed out.

We drove through Hilla and headed south down the highway to Najaf, which was only about an hour's drive. It was a little after four in the afternoon. Even though we were driving in a couple of the typical white Japanese-made king-cab pickups with the red racing stripes down each side, many of the children recognized us as Americans and jubilantly waved. It was the second day of the new school year in Iraq, and the streets were lined with young boys and girls in their school uniforms walking home from school. The television news played articles showing the students going through their text books on the first day and ripping out the pages with pictures of Saddam Hussein. The first page of every single book ever printed in Iraq during the last 25 years—including children's school books—was a full size photo of Saddam Hussein in one pose or another. In school books, it was usually wearing a suit and in some sort of "benevolent father" pose, while military manuals showed him firing different weapons, or in full military regalia. Between school books and military manuals, there weren't many other choices for reading in Saddam's Iraq.

As we approached the outskirts of Najaf, we passed by a huge cement factory whose smokestacks were churning out smoke, indicating that commerce was still alive and well in Iraq. By now, it was getting dark. Even Iraq practiced some sort of daylight savings time, and on October 1, we all had to turn our clocks back one hour, resulting in earlier sunrises and sunsets.

Tactical Human Intelligence (HUMINT) Team (THT) 108 currently consisted of five Soldiers and two interpreters, or "terps,"—they were native-born Iraqis who had emigrated to the States several years ago and had become U.S. citizens. Both were practicing *Shi'ite* Muslims, and were married with children. Mohammed, who everyone called Moe, was tall and thin, with short-cropped hair and a five o'clock shadow. He had been born around Basra in the south, and had since moved to Phoenix, Arizona. Mike was about five foot seven with well-groomed short curly hair and a thin mustache. He was from Chicago, had been born and raised in Najaf, and still had many relatives in the city. He and other members of his family had fought against Saddam during the 1991 *Intifada* after the First Gulf War, and had to flee across hundreds of miles of open desert to Saudi Arabia, constantly dodging the Republican Guard that were hunting them. Standard practice during the *Intifada* was for the Republican Guard to roam the open desert with helicopters in search of fleeing *Shi'ites*, and douse them from the air with gasoline. Then the helicopter would circle back around firing tracers to ignite the fuel, incinerating the refugees alive. Men, women or children, it made no difference. After living in a Saudi refugee camp for several years, he had eventually emigrated to the United States. Mike had a number of cigarette-burn scars on his forearms that he never talked about. I suspected that he had probably been in the care of some of Saddam's finest at one time.

The terps had given each of the team members Arabic names that would be easier for the locals to associate with and pronounce. Jeff was a specialist in his early thirties. His new Arab name was Samiir, but we all called him Sami for short. Standing at only about five feet five and with a thin, wiry frame that topped out at only about 120 pounds soaking wet, he was not in the least physically intimidating. He had bright green eyes and an infectious machine-gun staccato-like laugh that could be heard from a block away. He was the consummate optimist, very strong in his conservative political beliefs, and not afraid to practically impose them on anyone at will, and did so with us on an average of once or twice a week, which only caused a number of us to simply roll our eyes and walk away. But probably most importantly, he had seemingly boundless energy and a tenacious focus that drove him to success, no matter how daunting the task. On the other hand, Sami was a lousy driver, and we razed him mercilessly about his poor driving habits and his constant unconscious attempts to get us all killed on the already copiously dangerous roads of Iraq, where we observed traffic accidents on an almost daily basis.

Jessica was a specialist in her mid-twenties. She was now Leyla. She was the sole female on the team, but had no trouble pulling her weight with and standing toe-to-toe the rest of the guys. Her Irish-red hair and sky-blue eyes never failed to draw undue attention wherever the team went. She also had a real soft spot for animals. She had initiated the adoption of a stray pup shortly after the company had entered Iraq. The black-and-white female mix was named 'Bandit' after our unit's unofficial nickname, and became our mascot. Despite the restrictions imposed at the time by General Order #1 about adopting local animals as mascots, we had smuggled Bandit with us from northern Iraq to Camp Babylon, and then to Najaf, where Leyla was caring for her until Bandit could be processed and sent back to the States.

Mike was a sergeant in his late thirties, and the most mature person on the team after me. Since one of our terps was also named Mike, our Mike was now Yousef, or Joe. With his well-kept light-brown hair and chiseled tan face, he had the looks and smooth-talking skills of a well-seasoned politician. Back in the States, Joe was a senior manager for a major supermarket chain.

Paul was a specialist in his mid-thirties, and a county police officer. He was still called Paul, which was also an Arabic name. Paul had unique Filipino-Italian features and a quiet voice that still demanded your attention when he spoke. His police-officer demeanor meant that he usually expected to get things his way. He was never without a paperback book either stashed in one of his cargo pockets or open in his hand. He devoured detective and spy novels, and anything else we could get our hands on, in between pumping as much iron as he could in our makeshift weight room, which was actually in the driveway. Years of working undercover narcotics had honed his street-smart instincts for sensing trouble before it broke out. His nose for smelling when something just wasn't right kept us all out of potentially dangerous situations, and saved our team's collective asses more than once.

The current team sergeant, Kinysha, was re-named Samira. She had previously served 11 months in Germany after 9-11, and was due for early REFRAD (Release From Active Duty) within the next four weeks or so. Because of her earlier service, she had been left behind in Kuwait when the company had entered Iraq. At the time, it was unknown whether she and the other previously-deployed Soldiers would be sent home early or not, so it was decided to not penalize them unnecessarily by bringing them with us into Iraq if they might be sent home early. As it had turned out, they were all sent into Iraq anyway. They joined up with us several weeks later, after we had adopted Bandit. While the rest of us had bonded with each other as well as with Bandit, the Soldiers that had come later had been left out of that experience. This proved later to be one of the main issues that I would have to contend with.

Demographically, our team was mature for their ranks,

which was typical of most Reserve Soldiers. For a while there would be eight of us, until Samira rotated out.

As we drove through the front gate of the technical university compound where our base was, there were two older Iraqi gentlemen sitting in chairs next to the gate. They smiled and waved at us as we drove in. Sami explained, "Those two old men are always there, day or night, it doesn't matter. They're like the security guards, but aren't. They know everybody here. They're kinda like the retired men that hang out on porches all day in small towns in America."

We drove past rows of duplexes. There was a small children's playground, and there were even children playing in it. There were Iraqi families here and there walking on the sidewalks, many who smiled and waved as we drove past.

We weaved around a number of gravel-filled barriers and came to a second gate that was manned by some of the hired Iraqi guards. Each vehicle had a pass that we had to show in order to gain entry into our part of the compound, which was completely wired off from the rest of the campus with rolls of concertina wire and other barriers. The guards were armed with AK-47s. Once they had checked our passes, they raised the bar over the gate, and we drove in.

THT 108 lived in the housing area on the campus of a technical university on the southern edge of the city. The housing area was for the university staff and faculty members, many of whom were still living in the rest of the neighborhood. The U.S. military had occupied the last row of houses in the back of the living compound. The entire campus was ringed with a security fence, and there were guard towers around the perimeter, manned by locally-hired Iraqis who were vetted and trained by the U.S. Special Forces team that maintained the safe house complex.

There was a second inner gate manned by some Soldiers from the 10th Mountain Division (10MD). Just inside this gate was a sandbag bunker with a sand-colored 7.62-millimeter

M240 machine gun. The soldier there raised the bar across the gate and allowed us entry. The American compound comprised the last street in the living complex, and had eight duplexes. There was the detachment from the 10MD, another from a signal detachment providing communications and connectivity to the tenants, U.S. Army Special Forces Operational Detachment Alpha (ODA) 532, and an Other Governmental Agency (OGA) element. ODA 532 had just arrived a couple of weeks prior, backfilling another ODA that had rotated back to the States after only *four months* in Iraq. With the rest of us having to stay for an entire year, some Soldiers were resentful of the disparity. But then again, the Special Forces deployed twice as often.

The acronym OGA seemed generic on the face of it, which was just the way the Central Intelligence Agency (CIA) wanted it. After the "outing" of former CIA employee Valerie Plame by the liberal press, everyone was conditioned to substitute the term "OGA." Those three letters, CIA, when uttered aloud, drew immediate attention from anyone within earshot. No matter which country in the world you were in, everyone knew what "CIA" stood for. And because of the nature of their work, they naturally wanted to shun any such attention.

We parked our trucks in front of our duplex, backing them in up against the compound wall for a quick getaway if ever necessary, and unloaded my equipment. The duplexes were the nicest accommodations I had stayed in yet in Iraq. Each duplex had a small walled compound around it with a wide gate and a carport inside the compound. Since our entire complex was already double-secured, the carport area was covered with a camouflage net and used as an outdoor break area to sit and relax, and for lifting weights. I didn't realize it yet, but I had just become the highest ranking U.S. military intelligence officer assigned to the entire Najaf province—not that it seemed to matter much.

After my bags had been unloaded, we jumped back in

our trucks and headed into town to pick up some dinner. The streets were bustling after dark, filled with all sorts of vehicles. The people came out for all sorts of reasons in the evenings, and they were everywhere. They would shop in the markets, socialize, and eat in the many restaurants. It was even busier than usual now because there were busloads of Iranians making their pilgrimages to the holy *Shi'a* shrines here in Najaf, and in Karbala, another hour's drive further north. This had been the first real opportunity for Iranian citizens to visit these holy sites since before the Iran-Iraq War. They were thrilled to have this opportunity now.

The pilgrims posed a security problem that was not being addressed. Iranian intelligence agents were most certainly infiltrating Iraq posing as pilgrims. There was no way for us to discern who was an innocent pilgrim or who was an agent, so we had to treat all encounters with Iranian pilgrims with suspicion.

We went to one of the team's favorite restaurants, a place that they had nicknamed "Ugly's," because that is what the Arabic sign looked like it said in English if you read it from right to left, which was how Arabic was read. It was on a busy market street. We parked nearby and walked up to the entrance.

The restaurant inside and the street outside were teeming with people. One Iraqi man walked right up to me and introduced himself to me in fairly decent English, "Good evening, sir. I am Mohammed." He continued that he had two young sons named Mohammed and Ali. He had one wife, and one girlfriend, who he was working on to become his second wife, a routine which by western standards would normally seem adulterous, but was a normal part of Islamic culture, where plural marriage was not only legal but encouraged.

I joked with him, "While it may at times be nice to have more than one wife, one was more than enough to handle, and more would just end up a burden in the long run."

Then he changed the subject and made an interesting request, "Please get rid of Muqtada al-Sadr."

"Well, sir, that's really up to you and your people. The best way to do that would probably be to just ignore him," I replied. We would learn later that it would take much more than just ignoring him.

Sadr was the firebrand cleric that was causing all sorts of trouble in Najaf for the Coalition. Najaf was ground zero in a theological struggle over the Iraqi *Shi'ites*, and it was being waged throughout *Shi'a*-dominated southern Iraq, from the slums of Baghdad to the southern port of Basra. It was rumored that Sadr was the one behind the assassination bombing of Ayatollah ("sign of Allah") Hakim back in August, 2003, but was later discovered to have been the work of Al Qaeda in Mesopotamia. However, Sadr did order the assassination of rival cleric and son of another Grand Ayatollah, Sayyid Abdul Majid al-Khoei at the *Imam Ali* shrine's front gate back in April. In fact, an Iraqi judge had issued an arrest warrant against Sadr for Khoei's murder. Khoei had been serving a self-imposed exile from Saddam for many years in London. With Saddam in hiding, the U.S. Government had flown Khoei from London to Iraq, hoping that his moderate positions would help calm Iraqi *Shi'ite* dispositions.

Sadr's current main antagonist was Grand Ayatollah Ali Taki al-Sistani, who lived isolated in a small building near the shrine. When American forces had entered Najaf during the war, Sistani had instructed his followers not to oppose them. When he was criticized by Iraqi extremists, he issued a denial. Trying to keep the peace and not lose his influence, Sistani found himself in a tough position, but he walked the tightrope deftly. Still, everyone understood his position to one of implied support for the Coalition. Shortly after killing al-Khoei, Sadr had his thugs surround Sistani's home and threaten to kill Sistani if he didn't leave Iraq.

The *Imam Ali* shrine was the heart of the *Shi'ite* holy city of Najaf. Legend has it that in the late eighteenth century, a caliph who was out deer hunting when his quarry stopped and stood transfixed upon a mound of dirt. Then the caliph's horse also stopped, and the caliph reportedly felt a deep sense of awe, although he had no idea what the mound was. He asked around and learned from locals that the mound was considered to be the gravesite of the revered *Imam Ali*, founder of the *Shi'ite* sect of Islam. The caliph sponsored the construction of a magnificent tomb over the burial mound. Later the brilliant dome was enhanced with 7,777 golden tiles and enlarged even further to incorporate a mosque. Ever since, *Shi'ites* from throughout the Middle East made pilgrimages to the shrine to pay homage to what they believed to be Ali's remains.

Sistani garnered the utmost respect as Iraq's senior cleric, but there was one problem—having been born in 1930 in the city of Mashad near the Afghan border, he was *Iranian*—Sistani was not even an Iraqi citizen. Sadr was able to play to the people's nationalism because he was Iraqi, and his family name was respected with *Shi'ites* across the country. On the other hand, while Sadr was a young seminary student, he was nicknamed "Mulla Atari," because he preferred to play video games instead of studying the Koran.

In *Shi'ite* tradition, each believer individually chose a *marja-e taqlid*—a high-level and learned theologian—and obeyed his decrees. Currently, for most Iraqi *Shi'ites*, that was Sistani. But Sadr wanted the title for himself, and apparently wasn't hesitant to try to kill anyone that got in his way.

The Sadr family name had quite a respected history among Iraqi *Shi'ites*. In 1958, Muqtada's uncle, Mohamad Baqir Al-Sadr, had formed the Islamic-based *Dawa Islamiya* (Islamic Call) Party to counter communism and atheism in Iraq. In early April 1980, shortly after the Ayatollah Khomeini seized power in Iran, Saddam feared Khomeini's influence over the 15 million *Shi'a* majority in Iraq. Saddam asked Baqir, then the leading *Shi'ite* cleric in Iraq, to denounce Khomeini.

Instead, Baqir made the fatal mistake of publicly supporting Khomeini's public calls to "liberate Jerusalem via Karbala," which meant overthrowing Iraq along the way. Saddam had Baqir and his sister arrested.

It was unheard of to arrest a holy man in Arab culture, but this taboo didn't seem to faze Saddam. On April 8th, Baqir was tied up and forced to watch as his sister was brutally gang-raped by Saddam's *Mukhabarat* secret police thugs, and then she was ruthlessly murdered in front of him. Then Baqir himself was tortured, had his beard set on fire, and was also killed.

But Saddam wasn't through yet. He then threw Muqtada's father, Mohamad Sadeq Al-Sadr, in prison for 11 years. After he was released in 1991, Sadeq then established the *Hizb Hawza*, or Religious Schools Party, here in Najaf, where many *Shi'ite* Muslim clerics studied. He gained significant influence among the Iraqi *Shi'ite* population, particularly among the poor, and also developed education and welfare networks independent of the Iraqi government, and revived the tradition of Friday prayers for *Shi'ites*.

In 1996, Sadeq declared himself the grand religious cleric for all *Shi'a* Muslims in Iraq, and he became very powerful with many supporters. He preached his sermons at the historically significant Kufa mosque to overflowing crowds sometimes numbering over 120,000. While preaching, he would wear his white funeral shroud as a symbol that he was ready for death at any time, a tactic that his youngest son Muqtada would later adopt. Three years later, on February 18, 1999, Saddam felt that Sadeq was too much of a threat to his power, and had him and his two oldest sons, Mustafa and Mu'ammal, gunned down in a roadside ambush by his *Mukhabarat* agents. Although Sadeq was only 56 years old at the time of his murder, his flowing white beard made him look much older. Riots erupted across southern Iraq as Saddam demonstrated once again that he was not afraid to eliminate *Shi's* holy men he felt were a threat to his power.

Muqtada, the youngest son, was the last survivor of his martyred family's name. Still young and inexperienced, Muqtada stepped forward and attempted to fill his father's very large shoes. After his father's assassination, he spouted aggressive quotes from Medieval *Shi'a* sources with great emphasis and anger from the podium at the Kufa mosque. Even though Saddam's agents carefully monitored the Friday sermons, nothing was done to him.

Muqtada deftly maneuvered to inherit his family dynasty's mantle of leadership, taking advantage of the deep reverence that Iraqi *Shi'ites* held for his father's name and reputation, to seize religious and political power in Iraq. He was too young to be a cleric himself, and had no association with the *Dawa* Party. In order to be considered a cleric, one had to undergo at least 20 years of religious study in the *Hawzas*. As far as anyone could tell, Muqtada was barely 30 years old, and had never studied at a *Hawza*.

Shi'ite clergy rise through a rigorous system of tutelage and strict hierarchy. They pursue years of exacting study in order to reach high-ranking positions and gain respect from the community. As a result, many of them are genuine intellectuals. Muqtada had not even begun such training, much less completed it. He had gained little respect among *Shi'ite* intellectuals.

Instead, Sadr and his lieutenants made adept use of propaganda, portraying himself through the use of religious symbology as heir to a long line of *Shi'a* martyrs, tapping into the sect's central trait of dying for one's beliefs, in much the same way the Imam Hussein did in the seventh century. He leveraged his father's legacy to claim a position as a leader among the *Shi'ite* community. He gained additional popularity in that he never left Iraq to live in comfortable exile, as did many other clerics. He also claimed the title of *Sayyid*, descendant of the prophet Mohammed, which also garners significant respect among fellow *Shi'ites*. Sadr would later come to twist his influence over his young and impressionable followers to willingly die for him fighting against the Coalition—by the thousands.

Under Saddam—especially after he used Muqtada's uncle, Mohamad Baquer Al-Sadr as an example to the rest—the leading Iraqi clerics distanced themselves from politics in the interests of self-preservation. Now that Saddam was gone, that deeply-ingrained habit worked in Sadr's favor. Having never practiced as a clergyman, he had not developed any sense of distancing himself from political issues. He didn't hesitate to fill the vacuum left by the other clerics, reeling against the Coalition. The young and impressionable *Shi'ites* who had suffered so greatly under Saddam for the past 25 years flocked to him, hanging on his every word. After the Coalition removed Saddam from the picture, Sadr gained control of a number of schools, hospitals and mosques in parts of Baghdad, Karbala and Najaf.

Despite this, the Coalition leadership wrongly felt that arresting Sadr would have inflamed the situation and led to major demonstrations, falsely believing that Sadr was a "prominent cleric," when in fact he was despised by a majority of the *Shi'ite* population as nothing more than an irritant blowhard. It was a glaring example of how both our military and civilian leadership were culturally out of touch with what the people on the street were thinking, and this specific lapse eventually led to open warfare that could have otherwise been prevented.

DAY 147: MON 6 OCT 03

We drove into Najaf through the late morning traffic, passing groups of pilgrims walking along the side of the road carrying flags and banners. They were on their way to Karbala via Najaf for the annual pilgrimage. As was customary of the pilgrimages, they would walk the entire distance from Najaf to Karbala along the highway through the desert—a good 50 kilometers—to publicly demonstrate their faith.

We came to 1920 Revolutionary Circle, the main traffic circle of Najaf. Ahead was the Grand Mosque of Imam Ali. I could see the upper part of the dazzling gold-domed roof beyond the buildings flanked by two golden minarets, the towers where the calls to prayer are announced.

The Imam Ali ibn Abi Talib, who was the prophet Mohammed's cousin and son-in-law through marriage to Mohammed's legendarily red-haired daughter Fatima, became the fourth *caliph*, or successor, to Mohammed. Some followers— later to be called S*hi'i*, which means "supporter" or "party"— believed that only members of the prophet's family had the requisite authority to rule, and refused to recognize the first three *caliphs*, and that Ali should have been named *caliph* upon Mohammed's death in 632. Others, known as *Sunnis*, held that the *caliph* should be selected by the people of the community. The *Kharijites* were a third little-known breakaway sect that believed that Islamic leadership should have been conferred on the man who showed the highest level of piety.

Ali and the *Sunni* leader Muawiyah, surviving nephew of Uthman ibn Affan, the third *caliph,* battled over the leadership of the Muslim empire. The *Kharijites* condemned both sects because their actions did not fit the righteous model they expected of a leader of Islam. In 661 the *Kharijites* attempted to assassinate both Muawiyah and Ali. Ali was killed inside Kufa's sprawling mud-walled mosque, but Muawiyah survived to become the next *Sunni caliph*.

After Ali's assassination, *Shi'ites* in Kufa called for Ali's son, Hussein, to become their leader. In 680 on the broad plain of Karbala, just north of Najaf, Hussein and a small band of 72 warriors fought to the death against Muawiyah's Umayyad Sunni army of 10,000. Hussein's head was severed, mounted on a pike, and marched through every town and village back to Damascus, the new *Sunni* capital. Karbala then became

Shi'a's other sacred city just north of Najaf, with two similar holy tombs—shrines built over the graves of Hussein, and his loyal half-brother, Abbas. With Hussein's death, the split into *Sunni* and *Shi'ite* sects became irreconcilable. The *Kharijites* moved on to western Africa, where their sect is still prominent in Oman and Morocco.

Najaf then became the center of *Shi'ite* learning. Outside the city of Qom in Iran, Najaf was the foremost center of *Shi'a* religious instruction in the world. In fact, Najaf had been the center until Saddam had come to power, and then it had shifted to Qom at that point. The difference between the two, however, was that *Shi'a* thought and practice in Iran was very rigid and closed to any outside influences. In the *Hawzas* of Najaf, however, thoughts and perspectives were open to discussion and interpretation without criticism or ostracism, encouraging the free flow of ideas, as long as the cleric could vocally and logically support his position.

But Najaf's significance goes far beyond academics. Numerous other stories deepen the city's religious and emotional resonance. According to one, Najaf was the place where one of Noah's sons died as punishment when he didn't want to enter the Ark. Another relates how Abraham and Isaac eventually settled at that spot, buying a place called the Valley of Peace.

To the north of ancient Najaf was the *Wadi al-Salam*, the Valley of Peace, the world's largest cemetery, stretching out for over five miles, and filled with the ground-level stone tombs used for Muslim burials. The city's graveyards housed some of the sect's most revered leaders. *Shi'ites* considered it a privilege to be buried there, and families brought the remains of their relatives from thousands of miles to be interred, making Najaf the greatest necropolis on Earth. According to legend, Ali had supposedly said any Muslim buried there would automatically enter paradise. Not much more incentive was needed.

There was an entire economic system in the city dedicated to the receiving, processing and entombment of the dead, all accomplished within the three-day limit imposed by the Muslim belief. How those that had to travel from afar made the deadline, I don't know. Elaborate ceremonies of prayers, washing of the corpses, and grave digging were carried out by families that had performed such services from one generation to another for centuries. The families that provided such services had become quite prosperous—the continuous state of warfare throughout the Middle East across the centuries kept their services in great demand. For the morticians of Najaf, business was good.

Adjacent to 1920 Revolutionary Square was a large courtyard that was under construction to become yet another holy shrine, this one dedicated to Imam Hakim, who had been assassinated in the bombing on August 29. Underneath a large onion-shaped green dome lay on display what was claimed to be the Imam's only recoverable remains from the blast—one hand.

We turned behind Hakim's shrine, entering the compound of the Najaf Police Department. The courtyard was lined with a number of Iraqi police vehicles, and a few U.S. Army Military Police (MP) Humvees.

A young Iraqi had come to the station to provide information on the *Fedayeen*, Saddam's guerrilla army. The *Fedayeen* had tried to recruit him, but he didn't want to work for them. A few of our agents went inside and talked with him for a while to see if there was any valuable information he could provide to us about the *Fedayeen's* activities or future plans.

After the interview with the *Fedayeen* defector was finished, we went to get lunch from a small restaurant across from the cemetery that the team affectionately called "Red's," a nickname they bestowed on the restaurant's owner because of his curly red hair. We combat-parked our trucks facing the street, and Red came out to greet us and take our orders.

While we sat in our trucks waiting for our lunch orders, an Iraqi man walked over to talk to us, carrying his young baby daughter. He was a regular around Red's, and the team members had met him before. Sami explained, "This gentleman was a survivor of a mass grave execution by Saddam's *Mukhabarat* during the *Shi'a Intifada* in 1991 after the First Gulf War. He was rounded up with about 500 other residents of Najaf and marched out into the desert into a mass grave, and then machine gunned. He was hit in the shoulder, fell down, and was covered by the bodies of the other victims around him. Hours later, after the executioners had left, he dug his way out. He was the sole survivor. He has a huge softball- sized chunk taken out of his back and shoulder from the bullet wound." The man lifted up the collar of his *dishdashah* and showed me the gaping four-inch-wide depression in his back.

Next, the man's other daughter approached our truck. She looked about seven years old, and was very pretty with green eyes. "You know, it's amazing to me after living through an event like that, that he could start a normal life again, get married and have children," Sami added. The man tearfully thanked us again—as he did every time he saw Americans, Sami clarified—for getting rid of Saddam.

Shortly before our order arrived, a small bus full of Iranian pilgrims parked next to us. They acted like Japanese tourists, bringing cameras with them and snapping photos of everything in sight. They enthusiastically asked if we would pose with them for photographs. Out of a sense for security, we had to politely refuse. As Military Intelligence agents, we could not allow ourselves to be photographed by foreign strangers, because we didn't know if it would be later used by a foreign intelligence service to identify us.

We went to visit one of the many political organizations that had cropped up in town since Saddam was gone. We sat and talked with four men for almost two hours about the local situation in Najaf and potential threats to them and the Coalition. Their leader, who spoke passable English—they had refused to permit our own interpreters to assist because they didn't trust them—had prepared a list of talking points that he went down as he brought up and we discussed each item. In addition to requesting a primary school be built in an area where the next nearest school was over two kilometers away, forcing the children to walk four kilometers every day, they also requested that we provide them with weapons. We informed them that only Iraqi police officers were authorized to have weapons in Iraq. Besides, there was a police station directly across the street from their office. Their leader invited all of us to lunch at his home the following week, which we graciously accepted.

"Do you know Karl Marx?" he asked us.

"Yes, I have even read his book *The Communist Manifesto*," I replied. The book was part of my personal library collection at home.

"If I gave you a book written in English, would you like to read it?"

"Certainly, I would be most gracious, thank you." I presumed it wasn't the *Manifesto*, but I would have to wait and see.

We left the office. It was already quite dark outside. We headed home for the night.

DAY 148: TUE 7 OCT 03

We drove north on the highway leading out of Najaf towards Karbala, the destination city of the current pilgrimage activities in Iraq, about an hour's drive. Our mission was to drive to about the halfway point and count the number of pilgrims we saw walking along the highway from Najaf to Karbala. The previous Friday, Muqtada al-Sadr had directed his followers to make the pilgrimage during the coming week to Karbala, and Lieutenant General Ricardo Sanchez, the coalition commander for Iraq, was interested as to what influence he was having on the population. Some so-called experts estimated that there would be pilgrims numbering in the thousands, and some even estimated in the millions.

Sadr's influence was a point of concern for General Sanchez, because his Friday sermons preached against cooperation with the Coalition, but not to the point of calling for outright violence—yet. One example was that Sadr was telling his followers that the U.S. knew that very soon, practically any day now, the *Shi'a Mahdi* (the "guided"), the Muslim equivalent of the Jewish and Christian Messiah, was about to appear at the prophesied spot at the golden shrine in Samarra, Iraq. Supposedly, American Christians were bent on murdering him as soon as he appeared, and this was the "real" reason why the U.S. conquered Iraq precisely at this time. The moderate *Shi'ite* religious leadership as well as the Coalition Provisional Authority (CPA) led by L. Paul Bremer, wrongly chose to combat these rumors by ignoring them. Bremer, the self-appointed emperor of Iraq, kept a huge plaque on his desk in Baghdad's Green Zone engraved with the phrase, "Success has a thousand fathers." It seemed antithetical to Truman's "The buck stops here."

Ambassador Bremer worked for the State Department. Secretary Rumsfeld, who showed no love for the State Department, appointed Bremer to head the CPA. It was a temporary organization that duplicated practically all of the functions already performed by the U.S. Army's Civil Affairs branch. There was little if any cooperation between the CPA and the Army. Routinely, an Army Civil Affairs Team would visit an Iraqi village and assess the infrastructure that was in need of attention, such as the road networks, schools, water supply, electricity, and so forth, then develop plans to return in the coming weeks or months to make upgrades and repairs. Invariably, another team from the CPA would follow a few days or weeks later asking the same questions. The Arab community leaders would then think that the Americans must be idiots for asking about the same things that they already asked about just a few days ago. The whole routine went a long way to destroy what little credibility the United States still had among the Iraqis. This was just one of many examples of major conflict between the military and the CPA.

We drove up the highway from Najaf to Karbala, the route all of the pilgrims would be taking. We counted the pilgrims marching along the side of highway, carrying their green or black flags. They were in small groups, numbering anywhere from two to perhaps ten. There were even groups made up entirely of women, their black *abayas* billowing like large sails in the stiff breeze. Most were carrying bags with food and water in their hands, or put the straps across their forehead and hung them down their back. It was an awe-inspiring sight to see these people marching through the heat of the desert, trusting only in their *Allah* and the generosity of other fellow Muslims. All along the pilgrimage route, people would open their homes to them. Their children would stand on the side of the road with a bottle of water to offer them if they needed it. But out here, there was very little besides open desert for miles around. Despite this, they kept on trekking.

We passed herds of camels grazing on desert shrubs just off the highway. Just before reaching the halfway point, we encountered what appeared to be a highway rest stop, teeming with restaurants and auto services. At least a hundred buses and cars were parked along both sides of the road. Behind the rest stop to our right were the mud brick walls of an ancient fort, and beyond that was a village. We drove a little further north, and turned around at about the halfway point, counting only about 140 or so pilgrims along the way up to that point.

Next, we went around to locate possible *Ba'ath* party safe houses and weapons caches based upon information given to us by some of our informants. We plotted their locations using our handheld Global Positioning Systems as we drove past them for a safe and unobtrusive distance. There was one house in the city, and a date palm plantation just outside the city.

That evening, I attended the Governate Support Team (GST) coordination meeting held at the Tactical Operations Center (TOC) of the Military Police (MP) company on Camp Baker, the main Coalition base in the Najaf province. Camp Baker lay between Kufa and Najaf. There was a battalion from the Spanish army, along with a company of armored cars, which were the only armored vehicles in the province. There was an airborne infantry battalion from El Salvador that provided security at the gates and around the camp perimeter. American forces consisted of the Military Police company of only about 100 Soldiers, and a signals platoon of about a dozen more, providing communications and connectivity to Baghdad. The Spanish army also ran a Civil-Military Operations Center (CMOC) responsible for reconstruction throughout the province. Other than our own safe house complex, there was a Honduran battalion based on Camp "Animal" north of Najaf. This was the extent of the Coalition forces in the entire Najaf province.

Mr. Ford, the head CPA representative for the Najaf province, was present at the meeting. Also attending were the ranking colonel from the Spanish Brigade, the ranking officers from both the Honduran and El Salvadoran units, and representatives from Special Forces, OGA and the Military Police.

This was also where I first met Dean, the Special Forces chief, who was very friendly and helpful. The Special Forces and OGA didn't normally attend every meeting because they considered them a waste of their time, as nothing seemingly important to them was usually put out.

The first topic of discussion was the issuance of weapons permits to the Iraqis. At first, the MPs had issued cards to the newly hired Iraqi police officers, who were supposed to be the only Iraqis authorized to have weapons outside of their homes. Shortly thereafter, the U.S. Army Civil Affairs unit in the city started issuing out their own weapons cards to just about anyone who asked for one. And as if that wasn't enough, the mayor then started issuing poor forgeries of our cards to his own private army. Samples of each of the cards were passed around for all to inspect. It was decided that only the MPs would be authorized to issue weapons cards, and that all others should be confiscated on sight. There were two exceptions: the SF and our THT could also issue weapons cards to any of our informants if we felt that they were in danger.

The next topic of discussion was the discovery of some glass vials of an unknown substance by some Spanish soldiers. They believed that perhaps it was the holy grail of missing WMD, but after careful testing it was discovered to only be industrial strength epoxy glue used in building construction.

After the meeting, Dean took me back to the SF lair next door to ours and introduced me to the other members of ODA 532 and their two interpreters. He told me that if there was anything at all that we needed, just give him a list and he would see about getting it for us. The SF had so much money in their operational accounts that they couldn't possibly spend it all, so they offered to help and share when and where they could. When the topic turned to weapons, I asked if they happened to have any seized pistols. Without hesitation, Dean started walking towards the door and said, "Follow me."

We went to his room and he handed me a 9mm Browning Hi-Power that had been manufactured under patent by Fabrique Nacionale in Belgium. It had thick rubberized grips embedded with bronze medallions on each side, both bearing the Iraqi eagle and shield emblem. It was in very good condition, with a black finish and stainless steel barrel.

"We picked it up in a raid, and it's unregistered. I took it out and fired it just the other day, and it worked fine. I disassembled, checked and cleaned it. I'm sorry that I only have one magazine in it for you, but we should be able to dig up some more somewhere soon. Here you go. It's yours; you can keep it."

"Hey, one magazine is a hundred times better than no pistol at all. Thank you very much," I replied.

"I tried to make sure that all of your team members had pistols when we first got here. That's where they got the .380-caliber Berettas." I didn't care what anyone else said about Dean, he was all right.

Weapons had been another one of those sore spots with us. Our unit's organization only allowed each Soldier to be armed with either a full-length M16-A2 or an M-9 pistol, but not both. The M-16 was too long to wield from inside the cab of our small pickups, and a person armed with only a pistol in a real fight is just another person that needs to be protected by someone with a rifle.

We had seized more than sufficient quantities of folding stock AK-47s, magazines and ammo, and every team member was issued one. They provided heavy, reliable firepower, and were very maneuverable inside the cabs of our small Japanese pickups. In addition to being a larger caliber than the M-16, the AK was also capable of full automatic fire, while the M-6-A2 was limited to only three-round bursts. Out of necessity, I was now fully armed with all-foreign weaponry. My AK and Browning went everywhere with me, while my M-16 stayed in my room behind my door, locked and loaded in case our base was attacked. I would have gladly used an M-4 and M-9, had my own army equipped me with them. But my AK and Browning were satisfactory substitutes. The folding stock AKs fit nicely on our laps as we drove around in our pickups, making them instantly available if needed.

DAY 150: THU 9 OCT 03

We drove over to the Najaf Traffic Police station to meet with their chief of police. We had heard a report that a couple of his officers had been abducted and beaten by some of Sadr's thugs, and we were trying to find out the details of exactly what had happened, and determine if the situation required intervention by the Coalition.

We sat and talked privately with the general in charge of the traffic police and one of his colonels in an attempt to ascertain the details. After a while, we were able to make appointments to see the men themselves. We found it a bit amusing that everyone in Iraq with any authority had to be a general. Everyone else was a colonel, so if you weren't a general, you were a nobody.

That evening, the attendance at the CPA meeting was considerably lighter than the previous. Other than Joseph and I, there were the three ranking officers each from Spain, Honduras and El Salvador, and a couple of MPs. There was Sergeant First Class (SFC) Lombard, the MP company's operations and intelligence coordinator whom I had met at the previous meeting, and another Soldier sitting at the head of the table who for whatever reason had not been at the previous meeting. He was a black man, and appeared to be in his early thirties. He was not wearing his uniform blouse, so I could not tell his name, rank, or anything else about him, or even that he was an MP at that point.

The meeting started off with a discussion of how Sadr's thugs were still going around armed in some areas, despite being told not to do so. There was one house in particular in town where one of his lieutenants lived, that recently had about 30 or so men with AK-47s loitering around it. The man at the head of the table spoke up, "I don't want Sadr's men not to be armed in the street. If I hear about his thugs outside that house again with guns, I will rally the MPs and go disarm them, and if they resist, I will kill them."

I raised my hand to interject a point, adding that I agreed that Sadr's men should not be armed in the street. The man cut in, "That's what I just said."

"Oh, I'm sorry, you spoke in a double negative, so I wasn't completely clear what your entire point was," and then I went on with the rest of my point, thinking nothing further of it. When I looked back at him a few moments later, he had donned his uniform blouse, and I could see now that his name was Simmons, an MP captain. And he was glaring at me angrily.

A couple minutes went by as the meeting continued, then he stood up, walked over to me and said, "I want you to step outside with me for a minute." Oh, great. I could see this coming. What was this guy's beef?

We left in the middle of a meeting discussing important security issues for the city of Najaf, something both our units were responsible for. He ushered me into an adjoining room, and started off by asking who I was, so I introduced myself and offered my hand, which he took. Then he tore into me.

"What the f--- is your problem that you don't understand what I'm saying? I'm the commander of this MP company here, and I've been in the army for 14 years!"

I wanted to tell him that he had only eight more years to go before he had as much time in service as I had, but I figured that right now was probably not the opportune moment to compare service records with him. It was quite apparent from that one statement alone that I was dealing with a man that was suffering from a serious credibility problem and a lack of self-confidence in his abilities as an officer and a commander, otherwise the issue of years in service would never have even been mentioned. This guy was more concerned about his image and his ego than he was about the mission.

"You made me look f---ing stupid in front of my Soldiers! Do I look f---ing stupid to you?!" He was exaggerating, trying to make it sound like I had stood up in front of his entire company and yelled, "Look, your commander is a total idiot!" In fact, there had been only two other Soldiers from his unit in the room, and one of them wasn't even sitting in on the meeting.

It was a poor attempt to try and bait me into a confrontation, but I decided instead to play the reticent Soldier who had greatly wronged him, and beg for forgiveness. It was the only logical course of action when dealing with this personality type. Had I offered any other type of response than total contrition, it would have only made matters worse. After all, according to army regulations, a Captain still outranked a Chief Warrant Officer Three. But so did a Second Lieutenant.

Standing before me was a prime example of a man who, given a little power, intended to use every bit of it to manipulate everyone around him. His choice of words—the four-letter kind—only helped to confirm this. It was the last choice of vocabulary for a person who lacked any more mature way to express themselves.

"No, sir, that was not my intent at all. I'm sorry if it was perceived that way."

"Well then what the f--- was your intent? Huh?" He got in my face and continued to try to push me over the edge, but I wasn't falling for it.

"Sir, I was only trying to explain that I was not clear on what your position was, that's all."

"Well, if you're not sure what I'm talking about, then you're supposed to say that you don't understand, not make me look f---ing stupid in front of my Soldiers. You got that?"

"Yes, sir. I'm very sorry, sir." Then he just stood there and stared at me for about ten seconds. I could see the wheels turning in his head, searching for a fresh angle to attack me from, but I had left him with nowhere else to go. It was obvious to me that he was looking for a confrontation, but I was not about to give him what he wanted. I just gave him a broad smile in return, which probably just irritated him even more. I had offered a sincere apology. Now it was up to him to show if he was man enough to accept it, and refocus on our joint mission.

"OK, go back to the meeting then," and he ushered me back out. I opened the door to the meeting room, but he walked right on past and down the hall instead, not even looking at me. I went back in and sat down, trying to remain focused on the rest of the meeting. Captain Simmons never returned.

One of the other issues that was brought up during the meeting was a report from Baghdad that a number of .22 caliber "pen guns" had been purchased and shipped into the city. It was basically a single shot pistol that looked on the outside like a regular fountain pen. It's fired from up close, usually into the target's face, and yields a low report similar to a firecracker—basically an assassination weapon. They were being sold on the streets of Baghdad for about $300 each.

When the meeting adjourned about 30 minutes later, The MP First Sergeant entered the room and came up to me. "Sir, my commander told me to inform you that you are no longer welcome in his company area."

So this is what it had come to. His choice had clearly been his ego over the mission. I didn't give him the confrontation he had sought after, so he declared me *Persona Non Grata*. He had demonstrated clearly that he was not man enough to accept an apology, but would remain bitter to the end. One thing I was glad for: he was not *my* commander. Otherwise, I'm sure that given half a chance, he would have tried to crucify me. I shook my head in disappointment for the poor Soldiers that had to serve under this man's command. It must have been a living hell.

After returning to the house, a few of the Special Forces invited us out to a night on the town with them, such that it was. We rode in their brand new, huge Sport Utility Vehicles, as they were much nicer and roomier than our beat-up little Japanese pickups. It was my first time in civilian clothes since leaving the States over six months ago, and I felt a bit awkward. I left my Kalashnikov in my room, and stuck my Browning in my jeans waistband. The Special Forces were permitted to wear civilian clothes if their situation warranted it, and were even permitted to drive around in a single vehicle, while for security reasons, we always had to have at least two vehicles with at least three people in each.

We drove into town and turned left, heading towards the *Imam Ali* Grand mosque where Hakim had been assassinated by the car bomb in August. I had not yet been in this part of the city. We drove along the boundary to the cemetery, and then passed through a busy market area filled with cars and people. Once we got through the market area, we came to the streets around the mosque itself. The streets here were lined on both sides with buses from Iran, and Iranian pilgrims were gathered in circles on the sidewalks next to each bus, or even in the street in front of or behind their bus, just sitting around chatting with each other, or cooking over small stoves and eating some dinner. There were some people who were even sleeping on top of buses. Pilgrims by the hundreds lined the streets, all assembled peaceably for their religious celebration the following day. Many had traveled hundreds of miles over many days to get here.

Then we passed in front of the shrine, but still at quite a distance. There was a plaza that stretched for half a kilometer from the street that led to the shrine. At the end, the golden onion-shaped dome was ringed in lights, giving the whole scene a festive holiday atmosphere. But just to keep everything in perspective, there were three police officers with AK-47s right at the edge of the street. We waved at each other as we passed.

We drove around in a large circle, and came back to the market area from the other side that we had passed through earlier. From here, we drove straight down the main drag all the way to the Euphrates River. In ten minutes, we had driven from one end of Najaf to the other end of Kufa on the Euphrates, passing Sadr's Kufa mosque on the way. Between the two cities was a small industrial area, a hospital and some other government buildings, and the Governate Support Team (GST) on Camp Baker.

We drove along the river front where there were a number of riverside cafés. We pulled over and requested a table, only to discover when it came time to order that they had no food, only a popular Arab tea called "*chai*," so we got up and went to the next café.

Here, we were able to get a table from a family that had just finished and was leaving. We ordered *chai* to start off with while we waited for our orders. They didn't have chicken, so I decided to try lamb kabobs. After our sumptuous meal, we went back home, where I would soon regret my choice.

DAY 151: FRI 10 OCT 03

At about 0130, I awoke out of my sleep with a bad case of Saddam's Revenge. I took a dose of ammodium, and then tossed and turned the rest of the morning, too nauseous to sleep. By then, I was also too exhausted to be of use to anyone, so I had to stay behind on the most important day of the week, the day that Muqtada Al-Sadr gave his weekly sermon at the Kufa mosque.

The content of Sadr's sermons were of such importance to General Sanchez that he read our reports personally as soon as we transmitted the translation to Baghdad. Every Friday, our team would don civilian clothes so that we could blend into the crowd without drawing an inordinate amount of attention to us, and one of our interpreters would go near the mosque and record the speech with a small handheld tape recorder, as many of the other worshippers did. Then the team would come back and the interpreter would translate the entire sermon, which would then be transcribed into a report and sent up the chain to the general.

Sadr's instructions to his followers determined whether he was inciting them to violent action against the Coalition, or cooperating in the nation's rebuilding effort. Hakim had eventually come around to giving the Coalition an opportunity to prove itself, but then he ended up killed. Sadr, while trying to ride the coattails of his belated father, was more belligerent, but walked a fine line, not to the point of inciting civil war—yet. He was also still too young to be taken seriously as a religious leader by many Iraqis, especially the older population. Born in 1974 in Najaf, Sadr was only 30 years old at most; most clerics did not reach leadership positions until they were twice that age. He started his religious studies at the Najaf *Hawza* at the age of 14, and married his first cousin—a widespread Mideast tradition—five years later. Clerics gain recognition and prominence through the publication of meaningful studies. Sadr has none. But despite his lack of religious credentials, Sadr was bestowed the rank of *Hujat al-Islam,* meaning "a Sign or a Proof of Islam," the third rank from the top in the *Shi'a* clerical hierarchy. With no accreditation to show for it, the position was obviously political.

DAY 152: SAT 11 OCT 03

We went to the Najaf jail this morning to conduct a hostile interrogation of a local *Ba'ath* Party leader who was suspected of having committed crimes against the Iraqi people, as probably almost all of the mid-to-high-level party members had at one time or another. Some Iraqi citizens were claiming that he had identified some of their family members as traitors to the regime at some point in history, and they had then been taken out and executed.

We were directed to an office at the far end of the compound, a sparsely furnished room with a desk, a table and three chairs, perfect for our needs. The prisoner was brought in, double cuffed with black plastic zip cuffs, and put into one of the chairs in the middle of the room. Then everyone left the room to formulate their interrogation strategy while I stayed with the prisoner. I circled around him slowly, in an effort to raise his tension level, while he pondered his fate. He looked up at me and met my gaze, then after a couple of seconds lowered his head and eyes. He was a tall, thin man with a beard and mustache, wearing a dirty white *dishdashah*, and appeared to be in his thirties.

Sami was the team's interrogator, and this would be his fifth of the mission to date. As an interrogator, Sami was unique in that as far as the army was concerned, he was not school-qualified. He was assigned to the company as the unit's supply clerk, and had been in the process of cross-training to become a Human Intelligence Collector when we were activated, at which point he had only completed half the course. But it was the most important half, where he learned the basics and essentials of the art of interrogation: how to read your prisoner and determine his weaknesses before even talking to him, and how to smoothly run and orchestrate a variety of psychological approaches against your prisoner to break him down and get him to willingly cooperate with you. It was a subtle art where there were no hard and fast answers.

And Sami, being fresh out of school, hadn't had the opportunity to learn any bad habits, which ironically had made him one of the finest interrogators in the battalion. With the schoolhouse fresh in his mind, he would go straight down the checklist, making sure nothing was overlooked. As the battalion's senior ranking interrogator, I had evaluated all of them in preparation for the war that we didn't get to participate in, and he had proven his abilities under the harshest conditions I could put them through. In fact, he excelled where many supposedly qualified interrogators flopped. In my After-Action Report of the interrogation training I had organized and conducted while we were at Fort Dix for eight weeks, I had described him as follows: *His source control, recognition of source leads and implementation of approaches is excellent. He displays very good discipline and focus. His questioning is by the book right down the line, some of the finest of the course. Recommend he be afforded every opportunity to conduct interrogations...*

And so—with the blessing of the company commander and First Sergeant—he was. This was of course before the restrictions imposed after the Abu Ghraib incidents, where investigations determined that personnel that were not even interrogators were conducting interrogations. At this time, no such restrictions were in place. Besides, I was in the room with them the entire time, ensuring that everything was being done by the book and in accordance with the Geneva Conventions.

Sami also had other talents that he had acquired in his life experiences that gave him significant advantages over many of the other supposedly qualified Soldiers. He had worked for a number of years overseas for an international advertising agency, and was very people-oriented.

Sami had finished discussing his plan with Paul and Moe, and they entered the office. Paul went to sit at the desk in the corner, and quietly took notes of any of the answers that the prisoner provided. Moe took a chair next to the prisoner—not ideal, but still functional. Sami stood in front of him and immediately took control.

"I want you to sit up straight, keep your feet flat on the floor, and look at me at all times." There was a pause between each sentence while Moe translated.

"What is your name?" The prisoner told him. Sami continued to ask for other particulars such as his date of birth, where he was born, was he married, and so forth. One of the more interesting questions that we had to add was, "How many wives do you have?"

Then he got down to business. "Why were you arrested?"

"I don't know." It was the typical reply we had all come to expect. Everyone was innocent and had done no wrong in the world, and we should all be so fortunate to wear the same rose-colored glasses, right?

"What was your job before you were arrested?"

"I was a mayor of a small village."

"How many people live in your village?"

"About 3,000."

"How many members of the *Ba'ath* Party lived in your village?"

"We did not have any *Ba'ath* Party in our village." An obvious lie, because Saddam had ensured that the Party was represented at every level of society throughout all of Iraq. He had set it up like a hybrid of the Nazi and Communist Parties, fully integrated with every aspect of society in every population center down to the smallest village. Perhaps the only people in Iraq who did not have regular contact with any *Ba'ath* Party officials were the Bedouins, who wandered the deserts at will like the nomads that they had been for thousands of years.

The *Ba'ath* Party was organized sort of like a pyramid scheme, where each member had to work their way up a vast hierarchical pyramid of levels. Each level had to pay monthly dues to the next higher level, all the way up to Saddam, who of course raked in millions every month in dues from his own Party. He then used it to bribe others into loyalty to him, by buying German luxury cars by the boatload and giving them away to his cronies, even as late as up to a few weeks before the war. If you saw a black Mercedes or BMW on the road, it very likely had been a present from Saddam. The mayor of practically every municipality in Iraq was a *Ba'ath* Party member, and maintained a ledger of who owed which dues. Like the Nazis, their recordkeeping was thorough and meticulous, as it had to be for each party member's own protection. If a party member was suspected of skimming off the top, he had better have accurate records to prove otherwise, or he'd end up with a bullet in his head. Also like the Nazis, their precise recordkeeping many times proved to be their undoing, and was later used against them.

Sami backed off a bit and then switched tactics. "What is your wife's name?" He told him.

"How old is your oldest child?" "Is this child a boy or a girl?" "What is their name?" "How old is your next oldest child?" And so on, until Sami had a complete listing of all six of the prisoner's children's names, ages and genders, from as old as 13 to as young as three years. Quite a young family.

Sami moved closer to the prisoner, "Now I'm going to tell you something, and I want you to listen very carefully. You and I both know why you were arrested. Several citizens from your village have come forward and provided sworn statements to the judge that you pointed out members of their families to be executed by the *Ba'ath* Party. The judge already has enough evidence to sentence you for a very, very long time in prison. Now I want you think about how your children look right now." Then Sami paused for a few moments, giving him some time to ponder.

"Now, I want you to picture what you think your children will look like when they are as old as you are now," he paused for the translation, "because that is what they will look like before you ever see them again."

At that moment, the prisoner lowered his head and began sobbing out loud. Sami had done it: he had broken the prisoner. It was the goal of every interrogator, to find the prisoner's psychological weakness and exploit it until he would do anything to cooperate with you. What would for some prisoners take hours—or even days—Sami had done in only about 20 minutes, and without laying so much as a finger on him—by the book. I felt like a proud father.

Sami paused for a few moments, letting the full effect of his statement sink in, until the prisoner finished sobbing and began trying to regain his composure.

"Now, I can help you to see your family again before you are a very old man, and before they all grow up and forget about you, but in return, I need you to help me as well. You identify for me the names of everyone you know in the *Ba'ath* Party, and in return I will talk to the judge to show you some leniency for your cooperation, and get your sentence shortened."

Sami went back and forth with the prisoner for two more

hours, with the prisoner cooperating at some times more than others, but in the end, he came out of the interrogation with the names of seven other *Ba'ath* Party members.

Out on the streets of Najaf, Sadr's followers were passing out flyers to anyone from the Coalition. In very poorly written English, he encouraged us to leave Iraq before there was trouble. It was an ominous sign of things to come.

DAY 155: TUE 14 OCT 03

There had been a running gun battle most of the night up in the city of Karbala. Some of Sadr's thugs from his *Mahdi* Army had tried to take over the city, but only managed instead to get themselves cornered inside a mosque surrounded by a group of Ayatollah Sistani's armed security guards. Instead of going in and taking charge of the situation, the Multi-National Division Coalition forces in Karbala simply surrounded and cordoned off the area, and let them shoot it out amongst themselves through the night. It was reactions like that that lost all respect for the Coalition in the eyes of Iraqis.

The *Jaish Imam al Mahdi*, or *Mahdi* Army, had been named after the twelfth and last *Imam*, who was supposed to be Islam's Messiah, the "expected one," for whom they all await for judgment day. This illegal armed mob was made up mainly from criminals that had been freed by Saddam from Abu Ghraib prison as part of an amnesty shortly before the war—whose goal was to cause chaos for the Coalition once the Coalition overran the country—and also some of the unemployed and disaffected people in the population. Sadr paid them a small stipend from his war chest to maintain their loyalty. A large part of Sadr's funds came from visiting Iranian pilgrims, who donated huge sums of money when they paid homage to the shrines, probably unaware that their money was being used to buy weapons for a future civil war.

Before the war, the vast sums that were donated to the shrines were administered by the Iraqi government's Ministry of Religious Affairs, and were distributed according to a recognized legal formula, with portions for the poor, for reconstruction, and for the salaries of maintenance workers, security personnel and other employees of the shrines. Now that the government was gone, there were no controls as how the money was spent. Simply taking control of a mosque or shrine gave the occupant control of the funds donated there. This was Sadr's goal. If he was able to take control of the most popular shrines, he could gain access to millions of dollars in gold and currency, and then use it to buy his army to fight anyone who opposed him.

That morning, we went to the Governate Support Team (GST) to gather any information about what was going on in town. Dean and Greg from the Special Forces accompanied us in one of their own vehicles to try to get some information of their own, and then we would compare notes later. There were rumors that 200 members of the *Mahdi* Army had taken over a hotel in Kufa—armed with AK-47s, and that Sadr was on the verge of announcing the creation of his own government, an Islamic Republic just like Iran. Most likely, he was just a puppet for his masters in Iran, who were backing him and telling him what to do and say.

Iraqis, like most Arabs, were highly susceptible to rumors of conspiracy. In a society where people could hardly speak openly with one another without risking their lives, and in which the media was fully controlled by an unpopular regime, people sought out information from every possible source. The *Ba'ath* regime even created a special intelligence branch to intercept, counter and to spread rumors of its own. This characteristic of Iraqi political life had not disappeared with Saddam.

At the high-rise hospital immediately adjacent to Camp Baker, the silhouettes of a couple of men could be seen walking back and forth, and looking over the Coalition compound. It was suspected that they were *Mahdi* Army spies. The Spanish dispatched some of their own men to clear and secure the hospital roof. When they arrived, no one was there, and they took up positions of their own to ensure that no one returned.

A little later, the MPs loaded up all of their Humvees and weapons and surged into the city. We figured that they were going to clear out the hotel, but nothing happened, and they were back in time for lunch.

The intel wasn't going to come to us, so we made the decision to drive around town and ask some of the locals what was going on. We drove past the hotel in question across from the Kufa mosque, and saw that a large black flag with Arabic inscriptions was flying over it—the symbol Sadr had adopted—but did not see any outward indications of armed men. But then again, we weren't about to go inside, either. As we passed by the Kufa mosque on the main street, there were about five busloads of young military-age men just loitering around, but they were not openly carrying any weapons. They were undoubtedly some of the *Mahdi* Army.

Street activity seemed to be no different than usual as we drove through the city. We suspected that Sadr was staying at his brother's house in the center of town, so we drove past there. Sure enough, the road in front of the house had been illegally blocked with cinderblocks. There were about 50 men loitering around the front on both sides of the street, and at least a dozen of them were openly carrying AK-47s. There were also three news vehicles out front with satellite dishes mounted on them. We drove right past in front of the house. Surprisingly, the guards hardly seemed to even notice us. We drove down about a quarter mile, turned around, and drove right back through again from the other direction. This time, a few more noticed our presence, but took no action. I had the safety halfway off on my own AK. Had even one of them raised their rifle, it was very likely that there would have been lead flying in both directions. What was disappointing was that within sight of all of the activity in front of this house was the Kufa traffic police station, about a quarter mile away across an open field. At the station were parked three MP Humvees. So much for Captain Simmons' pledge to disarm anyone openly carrying weapons. It was no wonder that we had no credibility with the citizens.

Starting at three in the afternoon, the two Arab news stations, *Al Arabiya* and *Al Jazeera*, started carrying live broadcasts of Sadr at his brother's house announcing that he planned to create a new Iraqi government within ten days, and demanded that the Coalition announce a date as to when they would leave Iraq.

While all of this was going on, General Sanchez decided to pay a visit and tour Najaf accompanied by a major from each of the three coalition armies deployed in the city. He made no announcements nor issued any orders. I was beginning to see a pattern from our military leaders—a pattern of inaction. It was very frustrating and disappointing.

Sanchez made the statement, "We've stated very clearly over and over again that the standing up of independent militias is not an option here in the country. And we're going to take the necessary steps to ensure that that doesn't happen."

Unfortunately, his words proved to be meaningless, as *nothing* was done about Sadr's *Mahdi* Army, which eventually turned Karbala, Najaf and Kufa into ashes and rubble.

DAY 156: WED 15 OCT 03

The pattern was certainly broken this morning, but all that it accomplished was to ruin the life of a potentially good police officer, along with any remaining credibility and rapport we may have had with the local police. On the orders of Lieutenant Colonel Kim S. Orlando, the 716th MP battalion commander at Camp Babylon—a hundred kilometers away—the Najaf city chief of police and one of his majors were to be arrested on weapons smuggling charges and then taken to Diwaniyah, a city about an hour's drive south from Najaf where the Spanish brigade headquarters was, and held until Sadr himself was in custody. The mission was given to Captain Simmons' MP company, who requested that we handle the interrogations until they left for Diwaniyah later in the day.

There were about a million things wrong with this entire operation. Before I had arrived, the previous team sergeant, Samira, had the team working for the MPs instead running our own intelligence operations, as we were supposed to be doing. The MPs were even running their own confidential informants, which was supposed to be our job, not theirs. The informants were giving self-serving uncorroborated single-source information that the MPs were blind enough to act on, leaving a trail of destroyed credibility and rapport in their wake. We were supposed to be the ones that recommended to the MPs who should be arrested, not some garrison command-via-email officer a hundred kilometers away who had no idea what was happening on the ground. It was so bad that we would have to eventually disassociate ourselves from the MPs just to try to rebuild our own credibility. It would prove to be an impossible task.

The arrests were supposed to be kept secret, even from our Coalition partners, so no coordination was made. When the first police officer was brought to Camp Baker and taken to an empty room for interrogation, the Spanish commander went to Mr. Ford's office across the courtyard and demanded that the unauthorized Americans in his building leave immediately. Mr. Ford came outside and asked who had authorized the use of office space in the Spanish-controlled building without any coordination. He also wanted to know why he hadn't been informed of the arrests and interrogations, as he would be the one taking the phone calls and questions from the irate mayors and police chiefs about why their officers were being arrested. I simply shrugged and directed him to query Captain Simmons.

The interrogation ended before it began, and everyone

stood embarrassingly outside in the sun for about 20 minutes until a decision was made to go down to the MP company area—where they had no suitable interrogation room, just a space behind some stacked boxes of water in a large room and in a hot tent outside, which actually proved to be beneficial—and conduct the interrogations there. That was fine, except that Captain Simmons had declared me off limits to his company area, so I just sat in the truck for the day, no problem really, since I wanted nothing to do with this goat rope as it was.

How these particular officers had been selected for arrest and interrogation was a mystery to us. There were other officers that were known to be way dirtier than these, and they were still out there working as policemen. But we had not had any say in the matter, and were just along to find out what, if anything, they knew.

By 1000 hours, two carloads of local police officers had arrived to meet with Mr. Ford to ask about why their fellow officers had been arrested.

Over lunch, I met and talked a little with Sergeant First Class Lombard, the MP Company's operations and intelligence Sergeant in charge. "I'm disappointed that the decision had been made to arrest these two officers based solely upon one uncorroborated line in one report from one source," he told me. "My battalion's operating method is like a concrete fishbowl, unable to see out as to what is going on around them. Oh, and by the way, you'll be pleased to know that our battalion commander, Lieutenant Colonel Orlando, had given strict orders that our MP Company was *not* to cooperate with you and your Soldiers."

This was probably stemming from ongoing disputes with our own higher headquarters and headquarters personnel back at Camp Babylon, where even though we were neighbors, Orlando, for whatever reason, did not want any of our personnel associating with him. Sergeant Lombard was retiring in three more months, and was glad to be able to finally get out.

Our interrogations revealed only that the Iraqi police officers really had nothing to hide, and were not really guilty of anything serious, and that they were still loyal to the Coalition, even after being arrested. Unfortunately, even before they had been arrested, the decision had been made by Colonel Orlando that no matter what the outcome of the interrogations were, they would be incarcerated at Abu Ghraib until Sadr was in custody. This, unfortunately, gave us no bargaining power to use on them. We could not promise them that we would let them go if they cooperated with us, or if they were clean, as the case had been. It was a disappointment to us to see them go to jail.

On our way home, we drove past the *Samiara* hotel up by the Kufa mosque to see if there was any unusual activity. The large black flag was still flying over the hotel, indicating that it was still under the control of Sadr's thugs.

That evening, we learned that the generals had finally decided to take some action against Sadr's activities in Karbala. Sadr had ordered one of his lieutenants, Mahmoud Al Hasani, to take a unit of his *Mahdi* Army to Karbala and seize control of the holy shrines of Hussein and Abbas. The shrines had been collecting donations of money and gold for hundreds of years from faithful *Shi'a* pilgrims. Inside them were potentially hundreds of millions of dollars in gold and currency, with which Sadr wanted to build up his *Mahdi* Army. Then fighting had broken out between Sistani's guards and Hasani's *Mahdi* Army unit. Our Spanish Coalition partners, instead of going into the fray and killing the bad guys with the guns, simply cordoned off the streets around the fighting, and let them keep shooting at each other. The result was a Mexican standoff, with the *Mahdi* thugs holed up inside the neighboring *Mukhaym* mosque, with Sistani supporters in the surrounding buildings.

Because our illustrious allies in the Multi-National Division had not decisively engaged and stopped the fighting in

Karbala, General Sanchez had to order the 1st Armored Division—which up to that point was only responsible for Baghdad proper—to extend its Area of Operations to include Karbala, and begin moving heavy units there. General Fast, the division's intelligence officer, directed that the Karbala THT and our THT here in Najaf be supplemented with agents from other teams, with the expectation that with all of the activity in our area, there would be more work than we could handle. Our company headquarters generated a plan to temporarily transfer two agents from the Diwaniyah team to our team for the next 24 to 96 hours.

While it was a nice gesture, the general should have included the caveat, "if requested by the THT leader." We did not have any available living space for more people; I had occupied the last remaining room in the house. They would have to squeeze into the other larger rooms with our team members. Secondly, additional personnel only created additional logistic requirements, as our workload was not really affected by the ongoing crisis to the extent that we needed augmentation. But try telling that to a general. More is not always necessarily better.

Essentially, it just sucked to be one of those Soldiers who got to go on tour, and be dragged across Iraq temporarily. As it turned out, within 24 hours, our two visitors from Diwaniyah were moved again, right into Karbala, for a stay of seven-to-ten days. These poor Soldiers had not brought enough clothes and supplies for that long of a period of time, necessitating that their team make an additional trip through enemy territory to bring them the remainder of their wardrobes.

DAY 157: THU 16 OCT 03

Acting on a tip from the same informant as the day prior, the MPs took an Iraqi worker into custody for suspicion of providing information about the Coalition to Sadr's people. He worked for the Spanish in the Civil-Military Operations Center (CMOC) on Camp Baker. Again, the MPs requested that we interrogate their prisoner. This time, he was taken directly to the back corner of the MP company supply room, where a small space just the right size was cleared out for the four of us. And whether Captain Simmons liked it or not, I was going to conduct this interrogation, assisted by Sami and Mike.

We went over to talk briefly with one of the Spanish army officers about his work habits, to find out if there was anything odd about his behavior. Supposedly, this character would go over to the hospital next door where a couple of Sadr's men were spying on the compound from an upper floor office, and he would report to them everything that he saw and learned while working for us. The hospital spies had gained access to the hospital from one of the surgeons who was fond of Sadr and his views. Our forces had to date been unable to confirm any of this. And after our experience the previous day, this informant's credibility was pretty weak. But still, we couldn't take any chances at this point.

I began with informing him of the consequences that he would face for not cooperating with us and telling all he knew. He never wavered, insisting that he was innocent of any wrongdoing, and was loyal to the Coalition. After all, the Spanish paid him a salary of $75 a month, which was probably the most money he had ever seen in his life.

He was not confessing. We went back outside to strategize some more on what to do next. Despite our best efforts, he still stuck to the same story. We were beginning to doubt whether he was really guilty of anything.

When we went out into the foyer, Captain Simmons was there. He walked up to me with a stern look on his face and asked quietly, "What are you doing here?"

"Sir, I am interrogating one of your prisoners."

"And you're the only one who can do it?"

"I am the senior interrogator in my battalion, and the team leader of this team."

Then he jabbed his finger at me and started yelling at the top of his lungs, "I TOLD YOU THAT I DIDN'T WANT YOU HERE!"

"If you like, sir, I can pull my team out right now and leave you with your prisoner." He didn't like that answer, so went further on the offensive from a different angle.

"YOU EMBARRASSED ME IN FRONT OF MY SOLDIERS!!" Right now, he was embarrassing himself in front about a dozen of his own Soldiers with his wild and unprofessional tirade.

"And I apologized for that, sir," I replied in a voice even more calm than normal.

"WELL, I DIDN'T BELIEVE THAT YOU WERE SINCERE!!" This was a typical statement that people use when they just don't want to forgive someone. After all, how does one prove their sincerity? Did he want me to grovel on the floor at his feet and beg? I had been sincere, but if he had accepted any of my apologies, then he probably would have felt that he had somehow "lost."

"Well then I apologize again, sir." My reply had left him with nowhere else to go. He stood there for a few seconds, his eyes afire with anger, and I could see the wheels turning in his head, thinking where to go next in his feeble attempts to mentally push me further. Finally, he spun on his heels and stormed off down the hall towards his office. I went outside, where Sami had discreetly slipped out to get out of the line of fire.

I had now lost my ability to focus or concentrate on the real mission at hand. Sami understood what had happened and how it had affected me. I was supposed to go back in and take over the interrogation again, but he could see that now I was not up to it. We attempted to come up with a plan of attack for our next move.

Less than 30 seconds after exiting the building, Captain Simmons came back outside. He glared angrily at me, walked out about six feet, then turned and went back inside, slamming the steel door with all his might, making a loud bang, all without saying a word. He had just embarrassed himself again in front of another dozen or so of his own Soldiers.

We went back into the booth with the prisoner, and Sami tried a soft, friendly approach, trying to convince him that Sami was his friend, and that Sami needed his help so that Sami could help him in return. Again, the prisoner's story didn't change. By the time we finished four hours later, we were a bit baffled. We had tried just about every trick in the book to trip this guy up, yet he stuck to his story. Conclusion: he was telling the truth, which was supposed to mean that the informant who ratted him out was no good. We each pondered on our own for a while over the afternoon's events, and each of us individually came to our own conclusions that he had been sincere. It was the only logical answer. Despite our recommendation to release him, the MPs took him to the jail at Diwaniyah. From there, he was later transferred to the prison at Abu Ghraib.

CHAPTER 2
TAKING CHARGE

DAY 158: FRI 17 OCT 03

At midnight, the Military Police called us, saying that they had just taken an Iraqi into custody that had supposedly fired an AK-47 at the Salvadoran soldiers at the front gate of Camp Baker. Our team was dispatched to interrogate the prisoner, even though it had nothing to do with our mission. I stayed behind to monitor communications. They returned at 0330, exhausted and frustrated. There had been a mix up between the translations of Arabic, Spanish and English. The Salvadorans were not at the gate, but had been on patrol driving down the street. The Iraqi had not actually fired *at* the Salvadorans, but had fired into the air. After all, it was Thursday night, and every Iraqi with a gun fired into the air on Thursday night. During this time, I had prepared and sent an email to Captains Oliver and Dave detailing the problems we were having with the Military Police.

While all of this was going on, up in Karbala, the Military Police (MP) Battalion commander, Lieutenant Colonel Orlando, was out on the street with a patrol of his MPs, trying to separate the two factions that were exchanging gunfire. His patrol came across a group of *Mahdi* Army thugs carrying AK-47s. He ordered them to put down their weapons. As they laid them on the ground, Orlando began drawing his pistol and then fire erupted from the rooftops all around them. Orlando and two MPs were killed instantly in the crossfire of small arms from the right, followed by a volley of rocket-propelled grenades from the left, all fired from the upper levels of the surrounding buildings, and four more were wounded. They had been lured into a deliberate ambush by the *Mahdi* Army. The remaining MPs and Iraqi police returned fire, and killed a number of the attackers.

When Captain Oliver had read my email about the dysfunctional relationship we had with the MPs here in Najaf, and had also heard within minutes that Orlando had been killed in Karbala, he ordered that I immediately take command of the team here. My transition period was suddenly over, whether I was prepared or not. My instructions were to disengage the team from conducting interrogations of prisoners under MP control and refocus on our bread and butter: intelligence collecting and reporting.

We found out later that just the day prior, Lieutenant Colonel Orlando had visited one of the holy shrines in Karbala with one of the THT members from our team assigned to that city. While dressed in civilian clothes, he had gone inside the holy shrine and taken several photographs. On the way out, they were detained by a number of armed Iraqis who were on the verge of killing them at that time for "desecrating" their holy shrine, but the THT linguist that had been ordered by the colonel to accompany him had been able to talk the armed men out of it. Captain Oliver had become furious that Orlando had taken control of his team like that, and then put them in extreme danger. That evening, he emailed our own battalion commander, telling him that Orlando was acting like such a cowboy that he was going to get himself and others killed. Within hours, he had. Captain Oliver's statement had been sadly prophetic. Fortunately, none of our own Soldiers were involved in the gun battle in Karbala.

The change-over had been long overdue. Since joining the team, I learned bit by bit why I had been sent here. My first indication came when we had visited Camp Baker for my first time. After parking, Leyla wandered around calling for Bandit, the company's mascot. After several minutes with no success, she returned to the truck and began sobbing uncontrollably. I reached through the open window and rested my hand on her shoulder, and said, "I'm sorry."

Later that evening, Leyla shared with me what had happened. Kinysha had been calling our First Sergeant daily, complaining bitterly about the "flea-bitten mutt," and that it was a violation of General Order #1 to keep a pet. When the First Sergeant would no longer entertain her complaints, she took matters into her own hands. In violation of convoy security regulations, she grabbed Bandit, now pregnant with expectant puppies, and drove to Camp Baker. So that none of the other team members would be involved, she had one of the Special Forces Soldiers ride shotgun for her. Once at Camp Baker, she turned Bandit over to the MP Company's First Sergeant, who dispatched Bandit with his Remington 870 12-gauge shotgun, then dragged her puppy-bloated, bleeding carcass to the garbage pit. On the way back to the safe house, she wrecked the Humvee in a traffic accident.

How did Leyla know all of this? Kinysha cruelly told her all of the grueling details that same evening. Leyla had hoped that it was not true, but learned on my first day that sadly it was.

Sami told me while he was in the middle of planning and preparing for an intense interrogation of an Iraqi detainee, Kinysha had yelled at and berated him for failing to mop the floor. Sami was so rattled by her treatment that he lost focus, and was not able to effectively conduct the interrogation. Ap-

parently to Kinysha, mopping the floor was way more important than intelligence work.

He then told me about the time an Iraqi family had invited
the team to dinner at their house. Kinysha had turned them
down flatly, fearing that the family may attempt to poison
them. This was completely ridiculous to anyone who understood even the basic cultural fundamentals of Arab hospitality:
Arabs will protect invited guests with their own lives, and any
betrayal of such trust would destroy the family's reputation
among their own tribe for generations. Besides, establishing
relationships like this was one way we networked and got
information about Arab current events. Kinysha's unfounded
fear of being poisoned simply demonstrated her own cultural
ignorance.

While she attempted to hide it from me, I soon discovered
Kinysha's true interests, and they weren't collecting intelligence or accomplishing the mission. The night Lieutenant
Colonel Orlando was killed, Kinysha had spent over two hours
on the team's official Mobile Subscriber Equipment (MSE)
line, which is a type of field telephone, flirting with the First
Sergeant of the MP company. This was the same person that
she had kill Bandit for her. The MSE line was supposed to be
kept open for official business and operations. No one could
contact us while the line was in use, which is not a good situation to be in when you're in a war zone. Instead of conducting
intelligence operations, she had been using the team to follow
her boyfriend around under the guise of the team interrogating
any prisoners that the MPs had, just so they could be together.
Later on, I saw the MP First Sergeant running convoys to our
compound for the sole reason of meeting up with Kinysha,
putting his own Soldiers in danger just so they could hook up.
This situation led me to the conclusion that perhaps Kinysha
had her boyfriend influence his commander, Captain Simmons, to create an impossibly hostile work environment for
me, with the expectation that I would be sent back, and she

would get to remain there so that they could continue their relationship. Whether true or not, it was the only conclusion that made any sense, except that perhaps Captain Simmons really was an insane egomaniac.

That morning, we were expecting violent anti-Coalition demonstrations to erupt in Baghdad, Karbala, and here in Najaf, following the Friday sermon. The team usually went out on Fridays in civilian clothes. There had never been any trouble in the past, but now that there were rumors of violent demonstrations that would surely draw out Coalition forces, we wanted to avoid the possibility of mistaken identity, so we wore our uniforms, hoping that our presence would not stir anyone to anger. I also ordered the team to bring full battle load, all rifles, and our M-60 machine gun, just in case. Sami and I even pocketed a few grenades. If there was going to be violence, and the demonstrators came after us, we would need every bit of firepower we had. Especially since the police station where we stayed during the prayer only had one way in or out. If necessary, it would become our Alamo.

Personally, I was a bit apprehensive about the entire situation, and concerned for the safety of my Soldiers. As the team leader, that was my ultimate responsibility. With the previous night's violence, and the threat of more violence rumored to be erupting right in front of us, we all had reason to be concerned. Some of the other team members were nervous as well.

On the main road through town leading to the Kufa mosque, there were *Mahdi* army thugs along the street every 50 feet or so. They were dressed in all black, with a large round colorful patch on the their left sleeve that read in Arabic writing "*Imam Mahdi Army.*" They also were wearing white checkered scarves, which Paul mentioned they had never done in the past. Perhaps it was part of the plan, so that they could disguise themselves once the violence began. They were a stern looking bunch, mostly criminals and drug addicts, and other people unable to hold a steady job. These were the dregs of Iraqi society that no one but Sadr had taken in. Fortunately, none of them were openly armed.

When we reached the Kufa police station, I made a recon and assessment of the building to see where the best defensive position would be for the team. There was only a single steep and narrow stairwell leading to the roof, and the roof was the place to be to call for help and be possibly rescued by helicopter if necessary. I told the team, "If anything happens, the roof will become our Alamo."

Over the minaret loud speakers, an announcer was calling for all of the *Mahdi* Army members to assemble inside the mosque immediately following the sermon. That was a bad sign, as we knew that the mosque was where they stored all of the weapons that they weren't supposed to have, because they knew that the Coalition would not enter a mosque. Logic dictated that they were going to issue them out for the violent activity to follow.

The prayer started at high noon, as it did every Friday. Imams and Ayatollahs usually made two speeches during their Friday sermons: a political speech and then a religious speech. This was because it was a Muslim belief that religion and politics should be one and the same, which went to the root of many of the problems and differences the Muslim world has with western civilization, and the United States in particular. Sadr started with his political sermon. Our linguist Mike had earlier left the station and took up a position closer to the mosque with his tape recorder.

Once the political sermon ended, Mike returned, and we loaded up and left. The religious sermon was still to be presented, so we made it out even before the sermon was over. I felt relieved.

We were about halfway home when Paul remembered that he was supposed to meet someone right at 1300, the same time as the sermon was scheduled to end, and that he was supposed to meet him back by the mosque. We pulled over to discuss it briefly. I was on the verge of saying no, but no one else seemed to have any reservations. I gave the go ahead, hoping that if there was a demonstration, it wouldn't be violent, and that if it was violent, that we could avoid it.

We managed to make contact and get to a safe location where we could talk. On the way home afterwards, we passed by several hundred demonstrators, peacefully walking down the main street from the mosque towards the direction of one of Sadr's homes in the city. Following cautiously behind the last of the demonstrators was a group of Spanish army soldiers in their armored cars and armored personnel carriers. The crowd had been issued hand grenades to use if the Coalition interfered with their demonstration. As we passed in front of Camp Baker, the road had been blocked by a flipped over truck. The Spaniards were on site directing traffic. I wondered briefly if perhaps it was part of a setup to distract the Coalition, but nothing nefarious seemed to have developed from it.

At around dusk, the MPs contacted us, saying that they wanted to hand off one of their informants to us that they had been working with for a number of weeks now. We went to one location and met up with the MPs. Then I jumped into a vehicle driven by an Iraqi with some of the MPs and went to a house elsewhere in town to meet the informant. He was really cagey, fearing for his life from Sadr's thugs if it became known that he was working with the Coalition.

DAY 159: SAT 18 OCT 03

Things had heated up in Karbala since Lieutenant Colonel Orlando had been killed there.

An entire battalion of about 70 M-1 tanks had rolled into Karbala and were ordered to clean out the battle zone. Air support from A-10 Warthogs was laid on, and an AC-130 Spectre gunship was made available.

The leader of the *Mahdi* army elements in Karbala that had most likely been responsible for the killing of Colonel

Orlando, a man by the name of Hassani, became the number one focus of a manhunt in Iraq.

After coming back from another meeting, I checked by email, and found an urgent message from Captain Oliver that there was a chopper inbound to our location with an informant on board from Baghdad who claimed to know where in Najaf Hassani was now hiding. The phones had been down, so the email had been the only way to contact and notify us.

Once the phones were up and working again, I called Captain Oliver. The chopper was actually standing by in Baghdad awaiting my confirmation that their arrival had been arranged and approved on our end. I was instructed to select "reply to all" on the email message, as it had been sent to numerous people, and let all know that we were standing by awaiting their arrival, and then they would take off for our location. Flight time from Baghdad was about 30 minutes. It was already dusk.

The plan was to identify the location, determine somehow if Hassani was really there, and then send in our Special Forces neighbors to take him out, one way or another, alive or not. We pulled our trucks around back by the landing pad and waited.

After an hour of no chopper, we went back to the house. I called to find out what had happened, and was told that they would now be driving down. A little later, they called back and said that something else had come up, and that they would be down in the morning. Still later, they called back again and asked if we could go to a small town outside Najaf and conduct a reconnaissance of the town's hospital. It was rumored that Hassani's brother had been wounded in the fighting in Karbala, and was being treated in the hospital. It was hoped that Hassani would be nearby. It was a lot to hope for, but General Sanchez wanted Hassani, and was willing to have any and all leads pursued. Since it was already dark out, and we had never been to this town, we decided that we would go at first light.

As it turned out, we weren't able to continue this mission for three more days.

DAY 160: SUN 19 OCT 03

We went to visit the *Dawa* Party headquarters in town that morning. The *Dawa* Party, or *Hizb-Dawa*, was religious in nature, and had been one of the few parties that was not entirely wiped out by Saddam under his rule—as long as they did not demonstrate any political ambitions. Instead, they focused on religious schools and humanitarian projects.

The *Dawa* Party had occupied one of the former *Ba'ath* Party buildings in the city. All of the windows had been broken out, and the building had been looted and gutted down to an empty concrete shell. There was an armed guard with an AK-47 at the front gate, who waved us right into the compound.

We were warmly greeted at the front door, and escorted into the building. In the front lobby, we passed by a large fountain in the shape of an eight-pointed star that was no longer functioning. We walked to one of the back rooms that contained a large table and several plastic lawn chairs, and sat down. We were joined by a thin cleric with a white beard and wearing a white robe, who sat on the other side of the table from us. Another man brought us some *chai*.

The cleric told us that under Saddam, everything was run by family and tribal nepotism. There was a great need for social services in the city. *Ba'ath* Party members had committed many crimes and atrocities before the war, and the people wanted justice. We told him that witnesses would need to report those crimes to the special court that had been established just for such purposes at the court house so that legal action could be taken. The *Ba'athists* were quite disciplined at keeping detailed records of their activities. Unfortunately, because of the extensive looting, there were no records of the atrocities.

We discussed briefly about the upcoming local elections, and the cleric shared with us that the *Dawa* Party would accept the results of those elections. We all knew and understood that any truly democratic elections in Najaf would reflect the wishes of the *Shi'a* majority population anyway, so there was no real reason for them not to accept the results.

Next, the cleric told us that billions of Dinars were being fed into the *Imam Ali* shrine every month from the thousands of pilgrims that visited there. Pious Muslims were encouraged to contribute up to 20 percent of their income to the shrines. He was concerned that the funds would fall under the control of Sadr, and suggested that local committees be established to run the mosques and shrines in the city. We told him that we would pass on his concerns to General Sanchez.

DAY 161: MON 20 OCT 03

"We saw Muqtada!" Joe and Paul returned from lunch at Camp Baker, and relayed their encounter to me. "We drove down the alleyway past his house on the way back, and he was just standing in the doorway of the back gate to his house, right there in the alley. He was all by himself; none of his bodyguards were around! We just stared at each other as we drove by. I could've taken him out right there, and ended all of our troubles, and no one would have been the wiser!" Joe was excited about his close encounter with Sadr.

Sadr had two houses in Najaf. One was across the street from the town's children's hospital, and was always protected by about a platoon of *Mahdi* Army with guns and rocket launchers. They visibly roamed around the perimeter, but kept their weapons hidden but readily accessible in nearby huts and behind walls. While they allowed local traffic to pass by, it would have been suicide to stop in front of his house. We drove past every few days or so just to see what the current state of his security was like, but we had never actually seen the man himself. This was an unusual and noteworthy sighting.

DAY 162: TUE 21 OCT 03

We teamed up with the Special Forces and planned our recon mission. We had no idea what to expect in the town Ash Shamiya, south of Najaf. Would there be armed thugs roving the streets, engaging the first sign of Coalition Forces? In order to offer the greatest chance of success balanced with security, we decided to send in a couple of our native linguists in our most beat-up truck, dressed in local garb. Technically, we weren't supposed to task our linguists to conduct intelligence work like this, and we didn't: they volunteered. In fact, they had even suggested it. They were supposed to only translate for us, though. They went above and beyond, volunteering to put themselves in potential danger in order to keep us safe.

We assembled and headed out of Najaf towards Ash Shamiya, about 20 kilometers to the south. Along the way, Iraqi men were out in boats in the marshes along the highway, netting fish. Others were standing on the side of the highway holding some of their small fish up, attempting to sell some of their catch to passersby.

We drove to the outskirts of Ash Shamiya, where the linguists peeled off and went into the town. We continued on, then turned around and parked off the side of the highway near the edge of the town, and waited. About 30 minutes later, they emerged. We drove back to our safe house compound.

The town was quiet, and there was nothing unusual observed at the hospital. On the way back out, a column of Spanish army vehicles blocked the road across the street from the town's main mosque, and began directing traffic away and forming a perimeter. They were delivering a load of the new Iraqi Dinar notes to the local bank, replacing the Saddam Dinars.

U.S. forces started moving decisively against Sadr's men in Karbala today, mounting an operation to seize a mosque occupied by his thugs. While it was expected that there would be outrage and mass demonstrations about moving into a mosque, the result from the local *Shi'ites* was a surge in sympathy for the United States. It disproved everything that our leadership believed about the *Shi'ites*, that they would rise up against the Coalition and start a civil war if we moved against Sadr, but the opposite was true. Unfortunately, the message was lost on our leadership.

DAY 165: FRI 24 OCT 03

The phone rang. Sergeant First Class Lombard from the Military Police was on the other end. "I am instructed to invite you to a meeting with Captain Simmons this afternoon at 1700 (5 P.M.), if that's a good time for you."

"Sure, that's OK. Any idea what this is about?"

"I believe it has something to do with mending the relationship between our units."

"OK, tell him I'll see him at 1700, thanks."

All was quiet at the Kufa mosque this week. We went to the Kufa police station in our civilian clothes to get a read on Sadr's sermon for the week. Across the street at the smaller mosque, there were a number of buses from Iran that had brought pilgrims along to visit the city. Unarmed *Mahdi* Army soldiers dressed in black and wearing their name tags on their shirts, walked up and down the street, making their presence known and feigning to assist pilgrims.

At Camp Baker, I ran into Mr. Ford. He told me, "One of the city council members told me where Sadr's secret *Sharia* court was located, down by the Imam Ali shrine in Najaf. Do you know where it is?"

"We've already reported information on that, but since you don't have access to our reports, I'll tell you what we know." I proceeded to describe to him what we had learned from our informants about where the court was located.

"The Iraqi police won't go down there because they're too afraid of Sadr. I'm going to order the chief of police to go down there and close down the court, and if he doesn't do it, I'm going to fire him."

No one from the police ever went there, and the chief wasn't fired. So much for determination from the CPA.

At 1700, I showed up at the MP Tactical Operations Center (TOC). I was told that Captain Simmons was on the phone, and to please stand by. It was a typical power tactic, making the other person wait for you, because you were more important than they were, and your time was more valuable. As I waited, I noticed a new sign on his door that stated the following:

1. Come to the position of attention.
2. Knock loudly.
3. Enter when ordered to do so.
4. Come to the position of attention.
5. Salute and state your purpose.

That sign alone helped explain a lot about what kind of person Captain Simmons was.

Fifteen minutes later, he came out of the TOC.

"Hey, chief. Thanks for coming. Let's walk outside." We went to the door and exited the building.

Just outside the door, Simmons continued, "I wanted to let you know that I am willing to let bygones be bygones, and overlook our past, so that our units can work together again. It's important that the missions of our units not be hindered, and that we be able to work together, so for that to happen, I'm willing to let bygones be bygones," he repeated himself, as he extended his hand. It was blatantly obvious that he had been ordered by his commander to reconcile. I accepted his hand.

"Thank you, sir. It's very kind of you." Our meeting was over.

As we left the compound, Mr. Ford was in the parking lot with the members of his Personal Security Detail (PSD)—three MPs specially trained and detailed to be his body guards. Mr. Ford continued donning his ballistic vest as he quickly spoke, "I just received a report that one of my local workers, a man named Ali, has been snatched off the street by the *Mahdi* Army. I just wanted to let you know. I'm on my way now to see the governor to see if there is anything we can do. I'll let you know how it turns out." Then they jumped into their trucks and tore out of the parking lot in a cloud of dust.

Later, we surmised that Ali was our linguist Mike's brother, who worked at Camp Baker! Mike had already left for the evening to be with his family. We called him on his satellite phone, and he told us that on the way home, he noticed some trucks in his mother's driveway, so he stopped to see what was up. It was Mr. Ford, who was visiting to find out about Ali. After a phone call, Ali made it known that he was all right, and was up in Baghdad, and would be back the following day. All was well. It was never known where the rumor of his abduction had originated.

DAY 166: SAT 25 OCT 03

We went out on our first night recon in the city. We were encouraged to go out and about after dark to get the feel of the city at different times of the day and night. The streets were relatively quiet. Other than a random car now and then, traffic was practically non-existent. On a few street corners and in front of some open-front stores, there were small groups of men sitting around and talking with each other.

We pulled up to the Traffic Police headquarters, and noticed that there were already two Humvees with MP markings parked there. We parked next to them. One of the Iraqi police officers came over and greeted us, and we asked if he could show us to the roof of the station. There were a number of bunks outside the entrance to the station, and there were officers sleeping on them. We weren't sure if they were on some sort of on-call duty, or if room and board was part of the benefits they received as police officers.

We were shown to the stairway leading to the roof, whereupon we met the MPs. A couple of them were peering down the street towards Sadr's house with binoculars. I introduced myself. "Hi, I'm Harry from the THT. How are you all doing?"

The team leader, a staff sergeant, replied, "Hey, we're doing great. What can we do for you?"

"Well, we were here to check if there was any late-night activity in the vicinity of Sadr's house down the street there, but it looks like you guys are already on that."

"Yes, we've been doing this 24/7 for about three weeks now, with a new shift every eight hours, tracking any activity around the house."

"Have you noticed anything suspicious, or any regular or routine traffic patterns?"

"Naw, all we've seen is his own guards on their roof staring back at us with their own binoculars. Sometimes they even wave to us. It's apparent that they know that we're here and what we're doing."

"Are you able to keep track of any vehicles coming and going?"

"Well, once in a while, but we haven't really seen Sadr coming or going, except maybe once."

"Only once in the last three weeks?"

"That's right. Even with the binoculars, it's difficult to make out exactly who is who at this distance, and at night it's almost impossible. We have night vision goggles (NVGs), but the street lights in front of his house make them practically useless."

"I see. Well, it looks like you guys already have a handle on this angle. Thanks for your time." We shook hands, and I went back to the truck.

"It appears that our work here is already being performed for us by the illustrious MPs," I informed the other team members.

"How about we go drive by the Kufa mosque and see if there is any unusual activity there?" asked Paul.

"Well, since we're already up and about, we might as well. Good idea." We loaded up and tore down the street towards the mosque. There had been reports that the *Mahdi* Army thugs were training inside the mosque courtyard at night. Perhaps we could spot some activity.

We drove slowly around the mosque, but did not notice any unusual activity. The surrounding area seemed as quiet as the rest of the town. But that still didn't mean that there wasn't activity going on inside, out of view from the outside. We shrugged, and headed back down the main drag to the other end of town. Along the way, we saw some local friends outside in front of their house, so we stopped and visited with them for a few minutes on the sidewalk. Then we continued on our way back to our safe house for the night.

When we were almost to the other end of town, Paul said, "Let's swing by Sadr's other house out in this neighborhood." He got on the radio and informed the other vehicle. We had never been in this neighborhood before. We had heard about the house, but also that the street had been blocked off by some of Sadr's guards. Perhaps at night, we wouldn't be as conspicuous.

We pulled into the neighborhood, and turned onto a street that circumvented the small local mosque. Our windows were down so that we could enjoy the cool evening breeze, which we were unaccustomed to. As we drove around the mosque to the next street, we heard the loud shrill of a police whistle being blown from what sounded like the direction of the mosque's minaret.

"Did you hear that?" I asked Paul.

"Yes," he replied. We drove down the next adjoining street, passing an open lot on our right. There were about a half dozen men suspiciously loitering around in the lot. One man was standing at the edge of the street as we drove past. They all appeared to be wearing *dishdashahs*, and we did not see any weapons.

We screeched to a stop and allowed the rear vehicle to pull up next to us.

"Did you hear that whistle back there by the mosque?" Sami asked.

"Yeah," Paul replied.

"Let's get the hell outta here!" Sami exclaimed. Paul let his police skills take over, and he expertly sped the truck through the neighborhood, around another circle, and down a street that led back out to the main drag, leaving rubber on every turn. We went back home for the night.

We learned later that the whistle actually was a warning system used by Sadr's guards, and that they were in the process of arming an RPG launcher to use on us when we swiftly left the area. Without realizing it at the time, we had narrowly escaped our own deaths.

DAY 170: WED 29 OCT 03

Our safe house compound was on the edge of the city. Just to our south was a village that had a reputation for smugglers and other ruffians. Sometimes when we would go jogging around the back of our compound, they would take pot shots at us, or shoot at the hired Iraqi guards in our guard towers. No one had been hurt—yet. When the Marines had been here earlier, they raided the village to let them know in no uncertain terms that plinking at them was not acceptable. Now that the Marines were gone, the thugs were testing their limits again. Unfortunately, the SF team didn't seem very interested in taking any direct action, even though they had all the proper equipment and training for counter-sniper operations. In the end, I had to request from the MPs that they come out and run through the village to shake them up.

We went to visit the Najaf City Fire Department. Its proximity to the Kufa mosque made it a possible site for us to observe Friday sermon activity. While we were investigating the fire house, we noticed that there was what appeared to be an abandoned elementary school next door that was even closer to the mosque. We decided to use that the following Friday.

CHAPTER 3
DEADLY ENCOUNTERS

DAY 174: SUN 2 NOV 03

Soldiers of the *Mahdi* army were going out on the streets and making arbitrary arrests of innocent citizens, such as those playing dominoes or selling non-religious CDs. They were even beginning to arrest and threaten Iraqi citizens that worked for the Coalition.

DAY 175: MON 3 NOV 03

Najaf's chief judge, Muhan Jabr Shuwaili, and chief prosecutor, Aref Aziz, met routinely outside their homes on a sleepy residential street to share the short trip to work together. They had finished law school together in 1979. As Aziz backed out of his driveway at about 0830, he tooted his horn for Muhan to come out and meet him. Then from behind a bush next to Muhan's gate, and from the garden across the street, four men converged on them. Two of them grabbed Muhan, pistol-whipped him into near unconsciousness and then dragged him into the car.

The other two flashed their pistols at Aziz and forced both

men into the back seat. Muhan blinked through the blood streaming down his face. "Why are you doing this?"

One of the thugs cuffed him and answered, "We're doing this because Saddam wants you. Now shut up."

They drove off into the desert and shot Muhan to death while Aziz watched. They dumped Muhan's body, then blindfolded Aziz with his own necktie. They drove around with him for a few hours, then dumped him elsewhere in the desert, but left him alive.

DAY 177: THU 6 NOV 03

The mortar tube was aimed directly at the Governate Support Team (GST) building on Camp Baker, and was only 700 meters away, well within range. If it hadn't been for the chance passing of a Spanish army patrol, there may have been rounds going down range.

The building security guard had noticed three Iraqi men dressed in black, all carrying large black bags into the building and up the stairs. Just then, the patrol was coming down the street, and he waved it down. As the Spaniards went up the stairs, the three men slipped out the back carrying only one bag. When the Spaniards had reached the roof of the building, sitting there fully set up, aimed and ready to fire was a Russian-made 60-millimeter mortar. The only thing missing were the rounds, which were probably in the third bag that the men had left with. And to think that we had spent that morning at the GST.

We went to visit with the governor of the Najaf province. We stood at the entrance to his building as his guards took down our names. As we waited patiently outside the front door, a news crew approached the outer gates and started rolling film. There was a camera man, a sound man, and a reporter. We turned our backs, not wanting to have our mugs on someone's six o'clock report. But then, the film crew walked right up to the entrance where we were standing, still filming. I moved to the side while still keeping my back to them. When I was out of camera shot, I went straight to the crew.

"Turn the camera off," I ordered. The reporter immediately told the camera man, in French, and he lowered the camera.

"We are here to interview the governor," the reporter replied in a slight French accent. He started digging in his pocket and offered me a business card.

"Do you have an appointment?" I queried.

"No, we just stopped by to see if he was available." Funny, that's just what we had done, but we had arrived just ahead of them.

"You are going to have to wait," I said.

"We just wanted to film the entrance of the building here with all of the police officers standing here." There were now about a dozen or so officers lined up across the entranceway posing for their camera.

"I don't want you filming me or my people. Once we leave, you can film all you want."

"Okay, okay," he replied, and relayed the instructions in French to his film crew.

"Give me your card," I demanded. He handed it to me. The name on the card was Denis Brunetti, and it listed him as a *Grand Reporter* for *Television Française 1*. As I walked back up to the entranceway, we were invited in to see the governor. We quickly went inside to get out of view of the camera.

We climbed up a flight of steps to the second level. As we ascended, the film crew had already entered the building behind us, and was filming the lobby. We entered the outer office, and were ushered immediately through another doorway into the governor's office.

The governor was a tall, thin man wearing an Italian knock-off black pinstripe suit over a green dress shirt, and no tie. He looked to be in his early thirties, and was well-groomed. He wore a five o'clock shadow, demonstrating his personal struggle between east and west. His dress denoted his western orientation and leaning towards modernism, but all good pious Muslims wear beards. The governor met both east and west halfway with his short-cropped beard that looked more like three-day growth.

He greeted each of us and had us sit around his desk in the provided chairs. We introduced ourselves, and asked what his major concerns were. Without hesitation, he replied that security was his biggest problem. He had requested a security coordinator to work for him as an assistant to the governor, a retired Iraqi army colonel, but Mr. Ford had to approve him, and he needed a background check on the colonel first.

The governor could not get the police to do their jobs because there was no clear line of authority as to who they reported to. As it turned out, the chiefs of police in the province reported to the Military Police (MP) commander, Captain Simmons, the Coalition Provisional Authority (CPA) representative, Mr. Ford, in some cases their ministry departments in Baghdad, and also the governor. Because the police were accountable to everyone, they ended up being accountable to no one. It was the classic example of serving too many masters.

With the recent murder of one of the judges in town by unknown assassins a few days ago, there was a political crisis looming on the horizon of our province. The provincial government offices blamed the murder on the Coalition for failing to provide adequate security, of course. The government bureaucrats stated that they were going on strike, but in reality, no one could tell because most of the time they weren't working anyway. The governor told us that if the situation did not improve, he would resign. If he did, there was no one to replace him. The provincial council had not yet elected a deputy governor, and with the strike, there would be no election for a replacement.

The more I thought about it, the better it actually sounded: if there was no one left to run the province, then the Coalition could take total political control! The Iraqis had demonstrated enough that they were incapable of governing themselves, so this could be our big chance to make things happen! Alas, it was not to be, as Mr. Ford later convinced the governor to not resign. A few days later, he got the security coordinator he had been asking for.

DAY 178: FRI 7 NOV 03

Sadr's sermon seemed more militant this week. There was louder chanting than usual, with the typical chants of "NO, NO TO THE OCCUPATION!" "NO, NO TO ISRAEL!" "NO, NO TO AMERICA!" All the chants were repeated by the attending Iraqis at the tops of their lungs. We could hear it clearly through the mosque walls, and from across the courtyard and the street, over a hundred meters away. The really ironic thing was that on the following Monday, the Dallas Morning News printed an article that Sadr was becoming softer against the occupation. They had apparently not attended the sermon.

Another odd sight was that there were fewer *Mahdi* Army thugs on the streets than usual. Were they concentrated inside the mosque for some reason? We didn't know.

DAY 181: MON 10 NOV 03

At the gate of Camp Babylon, the Polish army had posted what appeared to be an upgraded and modernized version of the Soviet-designed BRDM armored car. The hull was basically the same, but the middle wheels had been removed, and a turret with a 14.5-millimeter machine gun had been added. It was quite an imposing sight.

The Spanish intelligence officers at the CMOC had been hard at work. One whole wall of their office was filled with maps and charts specifying every location and person that was associated with Muqtada al Sadr. There were photographs of several of his associates, as well as of his different residences, offices and vehicles. They were glad to share it with us in an effort to work together to take Sadr down before he instigated a civil war in Iraq.

DAY 186: SAT 15 NOV 03

We had received some donated school supplies in the mail from some generous Americans, so we went to another girl's elementary school to donate them. This school was in much better condition than the previous one that we had visited, and they were only a few blocks apart. The Coalition's civic actions efforts were beginning to pay off, though, as more schools were being refurbished around the country. This one was freshly painted and had good furniture. The only complaint was that they had no real chalkboards. They used sheets of plywood painted black, and the chalk did not show up well on it. The students in the back of the classroom were usually unable to see the writing on the board. We left our box of donated school supplies with the principal and took a tour of a couple of the classes. We left candy for each of the children to take home with them to eat after *Iftar* that evening, the breaking of the fast at sunset of each day of *Ramadan*.

We went to visit one of the local town's water purification plants where we had heard that there was trouble with the negotiation of contracts to complete a project to get it up and running at full capacity. While the details were hashed out inside the plant, a group of school boys gathered around our trucks outside. They were just thrilled to see Americans up close and personal, and that weren't intimidating.

It seemed at times that our job involved a lot of public affairs, with a little intelligence gathering mixed in. But that was the way it had to be at times. If the people were afraid of us or didn't trust us, then they wouldn't share information with us. We ended up doing a myriad of things that we had not been trained for as part of our jobs, but it kept things interesting.

On our way back from the water treatment plant, we drove through town and found a number of streets had been blocked off with debris. Traffic was already heavy from the religious events going on, coupled with the large numbers of pilgrims in the city. The roadblocks only made things worse. As we came to one intersection, we saw a half-dozen men in civilian clothes with AKs. In the background was one police officer in uniform. At first we thought they were all officers, but after closer examination of their identification badges that they were wearing on their shirts, they were actually Badr Corps thugs. They were working together with the police!

We went back to the GST to report what we had seen. As we were pulling into the camp, a platoon of three Spanish armored cars was rolling out onto the street. We went and reported immediately to the Spanish S-2, who acted surprised, and reported our encounter up their chain. Then we went to have some lunch in the camp dining facility.

After lunch, we went back onto the street. At the main intersection south of the camp, we spotted three Badr Corps thugs in civilian clothes carrying AK-47s gathered across the street. The street was four lanes wide with a tree-lined median. Just as we spotted them, the armored car platoon came up the street on our side. As each of the three armored cars drove past, I pointed at the thugs across the street. Each of the armored car commanders saw me as they drove past, looked across the street in the direction where I was pointing, then I saw each of them grabbing their helmet mikes to talk to each other.

The armored cars entered the intersection thirty meters down the street. The other side was blocked with large rocks. Two of the thugs took off down the street, while the third continued to sit in his chair with his back to all of the activity. The armored cars turned and pivoted, found the lowest spot, and climbed over the roadblock. The first armored car pulled into the intersection directly across from us where the lone thug still sat in his chair. The second armored car tore off down the street after the other two derelicts, but they had already ducked into an alley and were hiding in an unknown location.

The third armored car pulled up on the near side of the first one and provided rear security to the scene that proceeded to unfold before us.

The rear ramp opened on the first armored car, and Spanish soldiers jumped out. With their guns trained on the thug, still sitting in his chair with his back to them, one of the soldiers walked up to him and nudged him on the shoulder. The thug acted surprised and stood up. The soldier asked the thug for his identification. The thug removed the identification card that was pinned to his shirt and handed it to him. The soldier examined it carefully, then handed it back and gestured for him to hand over his AK. The thug looked confused and demanded an explanation. A couple more soldiers gathered around the thug. The soldier demanded again for the thug's weapon. When he refused to give it to him, one of the other soldiers on his other side grabbed it from him. Then they started pushing him towards the armored car.

At that point, an Iraqi Police car pulled up next to the armored car and started to yell at the soldiers. It appeared that he was trying to explain something to them, but the soldiers insisted that he get lost. After about a minute of useless intervention, the police officer drove off.

While this entire scene was unfolding, there was a news photographer with a large black 35-millimeter camera standing across the street next to the third armored car, watching everything that was happening. By this time, we were all standing out on the street with our AKs in our hands, also watching. The photographer and his partner saw us, and crossed the street towards us. As they crossed in front of us, I asked them, "Can I help you?"

"National Geographic," the photographer said in English as he handed me the press card that was hanging from a chain around his neck. "Hi, I'm Matt. I've been in Iraq for about three weeks now, working on an article about *Shi'a* Islam for the June 2004 issue. This is my interpreter Farhad." Matt looked to be in his mid-30s, had black hair and a short-cropped beard and mustache which undoubtedly helped the locals to relate with him as well as for him to blend in a bit, was dressed in jeans and a black polyester jacket, and was wearing a base-ball cap.

We all exchanged introductions and shook hands. It was great to meet another American in this place who wasn't mili-tary or government. Matt asked, "Is it okay if I took some photos of what's going on over there across the street?"

"It's okay with me, but I would recommend you get per-mission from one of the armored car commanders first, so that they know what you're doing." For some reason, Matt decided to stay with us and continue watching instead going back over to take photos. Maybe he didn't speak Spanish. By this time, the Spanish had unloaded and stowed the AK in the storage rack of the armored car turret, and were hustling the thug into the back. Then they rallied together, rolled back over the road block, and headed back into Camp Baker to deliver their prisoner.

"Do you feel safe in Iraq running around like this with no bodyguard?" I asked Matt. He appeared a bit nervous and replied, "No, not always, but we manage. Sometimes the worst trouble we get is from the military."

"Well, you know that there are standing orders that the military is not to interfere with the press, right?"

"Yes, but it doesn't always work out that way."

"Yeah, I know what you mean. I wish you all the best, and I will definitely have to look up that June issue when it comes out. Good luck." We shook hands again. Matt thanked us, said good-bye, and wandered on down the street.

DAY 192: FRI 21 NOV 03

We had to find a new location from which to record Muqtada al Sadr's Friday sermon this week. The nearby school had been compromised and was just too predictable. The school security guard had shown up the previous week just as we were leaving—to courteously open the gate and close it behind us after we left. We had no way of knowing who else he could have told that we had been there.

We decided to try the Kufa city hall, about a hundred meters from the mosque on the east side, adjacent to the city's gas station. There was a long line of cars waiting for gas. The lines had been longer than usual in the past weeks. As we parted the cars to get through to enter the compound, a small group of agitated customers gathered around us to complain loudly about the long lines, the slow progress, and the general lack of fuel. I told them that we would look into it—the pat answer to anything an Arab asks you to do for them.

As we entered the city hall, there were about four security guards. Mike started talking to them, then embraced one of them, and began talking at length with him. "He's my friend from high school," Mike explained. It was always a surprise how many people Mike knew in the city. At the time, we thought that it always worked to our advantage, and opened doors for us. Unfortunately, we found out later that was not always the case. But for now, there would be no problem with us using the city hall.

DAY 193: SAT 22 NOV 03

We talked to a man today who finally got up enough courage to come and tell us about something that he had seen many months ago. He told us that shortly before the war, a large hole was dug with a backhoe on the outskirts of the city. Then, two brand new tractor trailer rigs showed up and parked nearby for the night, heavily guarded by Republican Guard troops. The next morning, a large crane was brought in, removed the shipping containers from the trailers and placed them into the large hole. They were then covered back over with dirt, and then a slab of concrete was laid over the top of them. After it dried and hardened, then the concrete was covered over with sand.

Then, construction of a building commenced over the site, but the war interrupted the completion of the building. The man rode with us and pointed out the location of the building, adding that every morning, another man in a red Volkswagen drove past the location to check that there were no changes to the location. The man believed that the buried containers contained chemical weapons. We reported the information he gave us, but as far as I could tell, no action was ever taken by the Coalition to investigate his claim. Oddly enough, I learned later that this was a common occurrence across Iraq for reports of WMD. One would have thought that with the emphasis on finding Saddam's hidden stockpiles, every possible lead would have been exploited. But that didn't seem to be the case. I would learn more about this later.

DAY 194: SUN 23 NOV 03

We went back to visit the Najaf city communications manager to get a phone installed for us. We needed a phone so that local Iraqis could contact us and give us information. Previously, the manager had been completely unhelpful, and had instead attempted to extort us. This time, we had done our homework and learned that there was no fee for the installation of a government phone—and we certainly qualified as government. Any attempt to charge us fees was actually going straight into his pocket. This time, we formulated a plan, and went in with an attitude.

Moe, Sami and I went in to the communications center. Each of us had assigned roles that we would each perform on cue. I led the way with my AK in hand as my symbol of authority. I always brought it to the first encounter with any person we were meeting, but after that I usually left it in the truck, unless I wanted to make a statement. Even without it, I still always had my Browning Hi-Power pistol on my belt.

We entered the building and went to the manager's office. He had not arrived yet—it was still too early—but his assistant opened the door and let us into his spacious office. Within a couple of minutes, the manager wandered in. He put out his hand, but I walked past him, shut his office door behind him, and blocked it with my foot so that no one else could enter. The stage had been set, and he already looked nervous.

He went to his desk, removed his jacket and sat. He invited us to sit. Sami and Moe sat in the chairs in front of his desk, while I remained standing at the door. He asked again for me to sit as well. I just shook my head no.

Sami started off, telling him that we wanted a telephone line for our house, while Moe translated into Arabic. Without hesitation, he said that the price had gone up since our last meeting, and was now 300,000 *Dinars*, over double what he said we had to pay the first time. This guy was incredulous. He and Moe started arguing in Arabic, while Sami and I watched. After about 30 seconds of hot and loud back and forth dialogue between them, with Moe getting increasingly frustrated and angry, Sami interjected, "Moe, is it time?"

"Yes." At that point, Moe stopped talking. Sami got up out of his chair, walked around the manager's desk, and sat right in front of him on his desk. The manager moved back in his chair, looking puzzled.

"Last time, we came here, you said we had to pay only 125,000 *Dinars* for a phone, now you are telling us it's 300,000 *Dinars*…"

The manager interrupted, speaking English, "Please, you do not need to sit on my desk," he stood up and gestured to his chair, "please sit in my chair."

"No, you sit down."

"No, please I insist, sit in my chair." It was apparent he was getting more nervous.

"Sit down!" Sami was getting more forceful.

"No, please sit in my…" Now he was getting argumentative. It was time for us to establish who was really in control in this room. As if on cue, Moe got out of his chair, and the three of us yelled almost simultaneously, "SIT DOWN!!"

Without further hesitation, the manger quickly sat back in his chair, his eyes wide, and Sami proceeded to tear into him. In a sterner voice than before, and without Moe translating, Sami got right up in his face and continued, "We know from talking with other people that it only costs 70,000 *Dinars* for a telephone line, but that doesn't even matter, because there isn't supposed to be any fees for a government phone, and *we* are the government! Who do you think pays your salary? We know you're trying to rip us off, we know that you've been providing free phones to *Ba'ath* party members, and we know that *you* were a member of the *Ba'ath* party! Now if we don't have a phone within 48 hours-"

"Okay, you will have a phone today," the manager interrupted. He had broken, and we had won. All Sami was going to add was that if we didn't have a phone, we would be back with police to have him arrested for his former *Ba'ath* party affiliation, but apparently it hadn't even been necessary to finish his sentence.

By now, a number of people had tried to open the door to come inside to find out what all the commotion was about, but I wasn't letting them in. When they knocked, I opened the door a crack and said, *"La,"* (No), then quickly shut it again. All our yelling had drawn some attention amongst the other employees in the communications center.

The manager made a single phone call, and one of his men came back to our safe house with us. Along the way, we stopped on Medina Street—Najaf's equivalent to *The Home Depot* where you could buy almost anything related to construction or home improvement; I bought a telephone for 12 American Dollars and some telephone wire for ten more. Within a couple hours, we had our phone line.

Last week, a unit from the U.S. Navy's SEAL Team Six from Task Force 121 had been in Najaf to arrest Muqtada al

Sadr, take him into Coalition custody, and fly him straight to Baghdad. The mission had been later cancelled by Rumsfeld because supposedly he was concerned for all of the pilgrim traffic in the city during *Ramadan*.

Six more former *Ba'ath* party members were assassinated the previous night by Imam *Mahdi* Army and Badr Corps assassin teams working jointly together. This was our first time hearing about such joint operations between these two organizations. It was very unusual, as these groups were usually rivals. The one common link between them was their sponsorship by Iran.

DAY 197: WED 26 NOV 03

Muqtada Al-Sadr saw an opportunity to take advantage of the current fuel shortage in the city. He sent 12 of his *Mahdi* Army thugs armed with AK-47s across the street from the Kufa mosque to the government-owned Kufa gas station. They told the corrupt police officers that were there to leave, and then the thugs began organizing and running the station. To their credit, they were doing a better job than the police, in that they were not overcharging or accepting bribes from customers, they were maintaining order with the long lines, and doing their utmost to satisfy the customers and get the lines shortened. In effect, it was a brilliant public relations move on Sadr's part. He was showing the people that he could run the city better than the Coalition.

It was our own fault, too. We, the Coalition, allowed the continued employment of corrupt police and other government officials. The locals wanted to fire and replace them, but we were under strict orders from Ambassador Bremer all the way up in Baghdad that no one was authorized to fire any currently serving government employees—even if they were corrupt. It was a ridiculous ruling, and made the Coalition look like we were all party to the corruption, and further demonstrated the lack of credibility that we had with the people.

It also flew directly in the face of his previous ruling under CPA Order #2 signed 22 May 2003 to dissolve the Iraqi Army because he felt that they were corrupt. Bremer later referred to this as "the most important *correct* decision made in the 14 months we [the CPA] were there." The policy was designed by Bremer, and was approved by the civilians at the Pentagon: Fife, Wolfowitz and Rumsfeld. Bremer felt that it was important to demonstrate to the Iraqi people that no matter what happened, Saddam and his cronies were not coming back.

Unfortunately, none of these civilians had seen it fit to ask the opinions of any of the generals, either here in Iraq or at the Pentagon. As it turned out, they disagreed wholly with the policy, and had actually been counting on using the Iraqi Army to pacify and reconstruct Iraq. CPA Order #2 had come as a complete surprise to the U.S. military leadership, who had actually been in negotiations with Iraqi generals when the order came out. Like the generals, National Security Advisor Condaleeza Rice and Secretary of State Colin Powell had been completely out of the decision. Almost immediately after CPA Order #2 was issued, General Tommy Franks announced that he was retiring. Then all of the other top military commanders that had served under Franks left Iraq, including our own brigade commander, Colonel Gary Parrish, who was replaced by Colonel Thomas Pappas, who later became infamous for events at Abu Ghraib. Command of Iraq was quickly handed off to the Army's most junior Lieutenant General—Sanchez—who didn't get along with Bremer. With Rumsfeld's creation of the CPA, authority in Iraq was effectively split instead of unified. Bremer and Sanchez had to *share* power and authority over operations in Iraq. It was an example of the old adage, "a house divided against itself cannot stand."

CHAPTER 4
GIVING THANKS

DAY 198: THU 27 NOV 03 THANKSGIVING

We awoke Thanksgiving morning to pouring rain. Instead of washing the sand and dust off of everything, it simply turned it all to mud. It clung to our boots in huge clumps and stuck to everything. Our otherwise clean uniforms became filthy within minutes.

We loaded up to drive to Camp Babylon for a company celebration for the day. One of our trucks needed some fuel, so we filled it with a five-gallon fuel can. Naturally, as we stood outside in the mud, filling the tank, the rain started pouring down in sheets, soaking our desert uniforms to the skin. In a way, after suffering through months of intensely dry 140-degree heat, it was like being re-baptized.

As we approached the bridge across the Euphrates River on the highway by the Kufa cola plant, several Iraqi men standing on the side of the highway tried to wave us down, and there was a line of rocks in the road. For all we knew, it could have been an ambush, so we became extra vigilant, readied our weapons, and sped past them to the bridge.

Within seconds, we saw what the excitement was all about.

There was a five-vehicle pile-up in the middle of the bridge. The rain had made the roads extra-slick, especially since it had been the first real rain in several months. The end-of-*Ramadan* traffic rush was on, as cars and buses filled the roads across the country, working their way back to their homes after celebrating *Aeed* with friends and relatives. In a way, it was similar to the increased travel in America on Thanksgiving weekends. Paul noted from his police experience, "You know, more Americans are killed on the highways during Thanksgiving weekend than at any other time of the year."

The smashed up vehicles consisted of two buses, two cars and a mini-van. Traffic on the bridge seemed hopelessly backed up, with vehicles filling all lanes of the bridge in both directions. I called back to Sami on the radio, "OK, here's our big chance to be traffic cops. Let's go, Sami."

Sami and I bailed out with our AKs and walked up a bit further to where we could see the accident area. I conducted a quick inspection of the vehicles. They didn't contain any bodies or injured people, so they must have already been evacuated, which also meant that the local authorities probably already knew about the accident as well. But unlike in the States, you couldn't just call AAA (the American Automobile Association) or a local towing service—sure, they existed, but we had no idea what their phone numbers were, or if they even had phones.

There was a path through the wreckage just wide enough for a single vehicle at a time to pass through and cross the bridge. There certainly were not any local police around, so it appeared that it would be up to us to get through the carnage.

The bridge was slicked with rain and mud, and jam packed with three lanes of vehicles and people—on what was normally two lanes on the bridge—all honking their horns and yelling at each other to move. "Let's start by clearing this side and getting our trucks through the passageway, then we'll work on the other side of the bridge," I told Sami. He went down by the entrance to the bridge and backed all further traffic from coming onto the bridge, while I got the buses and trucks off to one side back into a single lane. Eventually, I was able to clear enough traffic to get one bus through the passageway, with our trucks closely behind. But then there was so much traffic blocking the far side of the bridge that they could go no further. It was a classic catch-22 situation where none of the vehicles could move because they all blocked one another.

I moved through the wreckage to start working on the traffic on the far side. There was a man walking up and down the empty aisle of the first bus, as if he were looking for something. I had no time to deal with potential looters, and kept the traffic moving.

The jam on the far side was worse. The entire bridge was packed bumper-to-bumper with vehicles in all lanes from the accident all the way back beyond the bridge. First, I had to get some vehicles to move just enough to clear the vehicles out of the passageway, so that more could cross over to the other side. Slowly, Sami and I directed the cars, trucks and buses, funneling them one at a time into the gap and across the bridge, merging three lanes into one.

It felt a little like the scene in the movie *Patton*, when the famous general jumped out of his command jeep into the mud, broke up a fight, cleared a traffic jam and directed traffic in the middle of a muddy field in France in 1944. Here I was standing in the middle of a bridge in my desert uniform, AK hanging from my shoulder, waving my arms at drivers, signaling them to stop and go, and yelling at some of them when they didn't pay attention to my commands. Just like kids, some of the drivers would test the limits to see how much they could get away with, and I would have to chastise them and put them back in their place.

We merged the third lane into the middle lane one vehicle at a time, creating a passageway for our trucks and the rest of the oncoming traffic to clear the far side of the bridge. Throughout the process, the Iraqi drivers and passengers were smiling, waving and giving the thumbs-up sign to us. While there were short tempers, many more were glad to see that someone had taken charge to make order of the mess and get things moving again. What they didn't know was that our intentions were purely selfish, and as soon as our trucks cleared the far side, we jumped back in and took off down the highway. The entire ordeal had lasted almost 30 minutes. At least it hadn't been raining at the time, although Sami confessed that that he had slipped and fallen not once but twice in the mud on the bridge. We left the jammed traffic on the bridge to sort itself out and continued on our trip to Camp Babylon.

The Thanksgiving dinner at Camp Babylon's dining facility was to be the highlight of the day, and we had been looking forward to it for many days now. When we got to the head of the chow line, we were a bit surprised to see that there was a carving table with a red warming light. But that's not what was surprising: it had a slab of roast beef on it!

"Where's the turkey?" I asked. One of the servers pointed to one of the large steel trays in the serving counter. It appeared to contain some sort of meat-like substance covered in gravy. I was issued two small slices. Next came the mashed potatoes, and a heaping serving covered half my plate as part of the Army's "Stuff 'em with Starch" program, then another oversized helping of yams. Since it didn't appear that I had enough of the mystery meat, I also took a slice of ham.

Out in the dining area, the room had been tastefully themed with Thanksgiving decorations. There was a table with pies, but the apple pie had been so popular, it was already gone. I was fortunate enough to find some of my favorite, though: pumpkin. Unfortunately, there was one major required ingredient missing: whipped cream. Pumpkin pie just wasn't the same without whipped cream.

I found a place to sit in the crowded room full of loud and

obnoxious Polish soldiers who had no real understanding of Thanksgiving, and attempted to make the best of it. I tried a piece of the turkey loaf, and it had no real taste whatsoever. At that moment, while I sat there staring at the mountain of mashed potatoes engulfing my plate, I felt an overpowering wave of depression pass through me. Here I was, thousands of miles away from the safety of my home and the love of my family, putting my life in danger every day, and I couldn't even get real turkey on Thanksgiving. My family was home celebrating without me. At that moment, it seemed more than I could bear.

I wasn't supposed to still be here—none of us were. But thanks to General Sanchez, we Reservists were the sacrificial lambs so that the Active Component Soldiers that we had replaced could go home after only six months in theater, while he had condemned us to a full year away from home. I wanted to cry; I wanted to scream; I wanted to throw my plate across the room. I felt an overwhelming urge to go outside to the balcony along the bank of the Euphrates and empty my magazine into the water, and then throw my pistol in afterwards in a vain attempt to vent my frustrations.

But I couldn't do any of that. To demonstrate any aberration in my behavior would have instantly ended my career. So I sucked it up and just drove on, trying my best to forget about all of it. I had to continue to pretend that I was normal and that all was well. I ate the slice of pumpkin pie, then took my overloaded plate outside and threw the rest in the garbage.

In all fairness, the government had done their part in attempting to give the Soldiers a worthwhile holiday celebration. Unfortunately, in my case, it had failed. It was the first Thanksgiving in my life without my family. It was undoubtedly the worst Thanksgiving ever. And it wasn't even Christmas yet.

My team had no Internet access, and no telephones to call home with. Other units had both. We couldn't communicate with our families. I couldn't even mail-order Christmas presents for my own children. It was enraging.

In retrospect, I did have a lot to be thankful for: I was still alive, uninjured and in good health, as was my family. My mother, now twice widowed, and despite suffering from a rare blood cancer that deprives the red blood cells of their ability to carry oxygen—essentially, her body was slowly suffocating to death—was still able to go to school, hold down a job, and otherwise continue to function in society with minimal assistance from other family members. Despite my extended absence, my children were doing well in school and at home. Others were not nearly so fortunate, even to the point where some of their children missed their daddy or mommy so much that they required medication in order to continue functioning in society. My wife, despite all of the hardships posed by my absence, continued to hold everything together, maintaining the household, raising the children as a single parent, continuing to hold down her full-time job as a banker, and even volunteering as our battalion's family readiness group coordinator. It was beyond what she had prepared herself to handle, yet she still continued, if for no other reason than there was no choice. All any of us could think of was: only three more months to go, and keep driving on.

DAY 199: FRI 28 NOV 03

We dropped Mike off with his tape recorder on a side street near the Kufa mosque—he didn't want to be seen getting out of a vehicle full of Americans anywhere near the mosque. We were all wearing civilian clothes, as we usually did on Fridays, so that our activities and movements around the Kufa mosque would not draw as much attention from the locals.

We drove up to another smaller mosque on the north side of Kufa that we had heard had recently been taken over by Muqtada Al-Sadr to see if there were any indications of his having done so. Like the other mosques in the city, this one was surrounded by scores of tour buses from Iran and other cities around Iraq, ferrying pilgrims around.

As we slowly drove past the front of the mosque, vendors selling all sorts of trinkets and wares filled the sidewalks with their goods, trying to make a few *Dinars* off the touring pilgrims. An elderly Mongol-Iranian man walked past the front of our truck, passing by the vendors with indifference, the ornate green shawl signifying his pilgrimage status hanging around his neck. Most pilgrims wore the strip of green cloth, usually made from felt or silk, or other expensive material, and ornamented with Arabic writing, or even the outline of a certain mosque, using gold-colored thread or piping.

We drove back towards the Kufa mosque, and the traffic became heavy. It took a good 10 minutes just to drive past the front of the mosque, which was actually a good thing, as it gave us plenty of time to get a good view of the activity around the mosque, while the heavy traffic provided good cover for us. Because the traffic was so heavy, and with us staying in a middle lane, hardly anyone even noticed us, even though we were surrounded by Iraqis on all sides.

Along the sidewalk in front of the mosque, demonstrating marchers had gathered with a number of solid-colored flags and large paintings of Muqtada. With about a hundred followers, they paraded around the front of the mosque, then down the street and around the far corner, and into the mosque's side entrance.

At the corner intersection ahead, a *Mahdi* Army thug stood on the curb with an AK-47 in his hand. We drove right next to him, but he didn't see us. At the gas station across the street, a number of other *Mahdi* Army strongmen were still loitering around, maintaining their control of the station. As we drove past the station, another one of them stood at the edge of the street with an AK. This one did see us as we drove by, but he did nothing but look at us.

We drove down to the next traffic circle, turned around

and drove back through, and headed for Camp Baker to inform the Spanish about the *Mahdi* Army men with AKs in the street. When we went back out past the small mosque in front of the Kufa police station, there were two more *Mahdi* Army members with AKs standing out on the street, right in front of the police, who were not doing anything about it. We drove down the street and saw a Spanish patrol about a hundred meters away. We pulled over, and I told the Spanish soldiers about the two men down in front of the mosque. By the time they arrived there, the men had hidden inside the mosque.

We drove and parked around the next corner behind the police station, and waited for Mike to call us to come pick him up. By now, the sermon was more than half over. We had parked on the left side of the street; I was in the passenger seat of the rear pickup. Within a minute after we had stopped, a white four-door Japanese-made compact car with four men inside pulled up and parked on the right side of the street across from the front pickup. An Iraqi man dressed in all black climbed out of the front passenger side and jogged over to the passenger side of the front truck, and started talking to Paul. Then the man reached up to his shirt and showed Paul the identification card that was pinned on his shirt. He was *Mahdi* Army!

Next, the driver of the car, also dressed in black, opened his door and started climbing out, clutching an AK rifle in his right hand. Sami and I opened our doors and climbed out with our AKs in our hands, held at the ready. I reached up with my right hand and flipped the safety to full auto, and then re-gripped the pistol grip.

All of us just froze in place for about three to four seconds, looking back and forth between each other, seeing who would make the first move—and what that move would be. The man standing at Paul's window turned around and ran back across the street. Cautiously, I walked up to Paul's window, facing the man with the AK the entire time, keeping my own AK at my shoulder. As I reached the window of the front pickup, I noticed the tip of Paul's AK barrel pointing out the truck window at the man as he ran back across the street.

"What did he want?" I asked Paul, still with my eyes glued to the armed man in front of us.

"He asked me, 'Who are you?' and I asked him back, 'Who the hell are *YOU*?' Then he showed me his *Mahdi* Army badge pinned on his shirt."

Both men started slowly climbing back into the white compact. The two men in the back of the car had never gotten out. The car pulled forward and headed down the street about 30 meters, and just when it looked like they were going to tear down the street away from us, the car slowed—and began turning around.

Oh, shit, here comes the drive-by, I thought to myself. I pictured the car tearing past us with AKs out the window opening up on us as it went by.

I trained my AK on the car, tracking it as it turned around in the street and started approaching us. I started backing behind the bed of the truck, expecting them to open up on us with their weapons as they drove past. Everyone else on the team was doing likewise with their weapons at the ready, fingers on triggers, tracking the car in their sights as it began approaching.

The car accelerated, and the men inside were peering out at us with eyes wide as saucers. The car continued past us. Almost miraculously, no one fired. The car screamed up to the next intersection, slammed on its brakes to wait for oncoming traffic, then turned sharply left and out of sight, heading back towards the small mosque.

After the car had passed us, I lowered the barrel of my AK and let out a heavy sigh. I didn't relish the opportunity to take another man's life, but I had been prepared at that moment to empty my entire 30-round magazine into that car if necessary. In fact, I had had every right to have done so the moment the second man stepped out of the car with the AK in his hand, and no one would have questioned my judgment after the fact.

I replayed that moment over and over in my mind the rest of that day, and pondered and struggled whether I had done the right thing for the benefit of my fellow team members, having potentially put all of our lives at risk by *not* firing and taking the armed man down on the spot. Had I opened fire, surely everyone else on the team would also have opened up with their weapons, and all four of the men in the car would have perished on the spot. In the end, no one on either side had fired, and no one had been injured or killed. The only conclusion that I could come to was that holding my fire had been the right thing to do—but it had taken me all day with heavy contemplation to reach that conclusion.

We drove around a street corner and parked. Up on the roof of the mosque, a *Mahdi* Army member was walking back and forth with an Iraqi *Tabuk* sniper rifle, basically an AK with a longer barrel and a scope. We eyed each other cautiously. We drove further down away from the mosque to another side street and waited for Mike to call on the sat phone that he was ready to be picked up.

As we waited for Mike, one of our Iraqi friends drove up and parked. He climbed out of his Mercedes and ran up to our window. "I have been looking all over town for you. My brother was beat up and arrested by the police. They have thrown him in the jail at the Najaf police station. Please, can you help?" he asked frantically.

"Yes, but we can't go right now. We're in the middle of something, but as soon as we're done, we'll go there, OK?" Sami replied.

"OK, thank you!" he said enthusiastically. Then he ran back to his car and jumped back in.

The sermon had been over for at least ten minutes now, and we still had not heard from Mike. I dialed my sat phone, and he answered. He was already on his way. We drove down the appropriate side street and picked him up. Then we headed for the police station. The brother caught up to us in Revolutionary Circle, and followed us to the station entrance, where he parked and waited. Civilian cars were not allowed near the station because of the threat of car bombs. Several police stations had already been bombed and scores of Iraqi police officers had been killed in the country by *Al Qaeda* and the *Fedayeen* in an attempt to destroy those responsible for maintaining the law and order.

We walked into the station, went straight to the cell blocks, and asked to see our friend. The blue door to the cell had a small window with bars on it. The guard yelled his name through the window. I could hear the other inmates struggling to help another man to his feet, as the man groaned in pain. Our friend showed his face at the window. There was dried blood on his face that had run down from his hair. His face was cut in places where blows had landed. His left eye was reddened. The corner of his mouth was also cut, and three of his front teeth were missing.

He reached with his long arms through the small window and shook each of our hands, greeted us and thanked us for coming. We asked him what had happened, and he relayed through Mike that he had parked near a restaurant when he was approached by police who requested to search his car. He obliged them, but then one of the officers started speaking foully about his family and insulting his mother, who was in the car. When he objected, he said that the entire group of 20 officers attacked and beat him, then arrested and dragged him here for attacking the officer and resisting arrest.

Every story has at least two sides. We went upstairs to the MP office to get the other half of the story. As I opened the door, sitting casually in the far corner of the room pretending to read a *People* magazine was none other than the now-infamous Captain Simmons, the Military Police (MP) company commander. He was wearing his ballistic vest, and had his M-4 rifle tied to it, hanging across the front of his chest. His Humvee was not in the lot when we had arrived, so he must have conveniently shown up while we had been in the cell block area. It seemed too convenient to have been coincidence.

We shuffled into the small room. Our friend was Paul's informant, so as per previous agreement, I allowed him to do the talking. My role was mainly to jump in and provide added clout if and when necessary. In theory, we were considered Military Intelligence agents, and had special powers—under the right circumstances—to override even a general's orders. That was part of the reason why we didn't wear any rank, because it instantly advertised everyone's place in the military hierarchy. Unfortunately, my history with Captain Simmons was bound to taint his perception of any requests for assistance or cooperation from us.

"We would like to request that our friend be released," Paul said to the captain.

Simmons looked up nonchalantly from the magazine, "Why?"

"Because he's a very, very good friend of ours," Paul replied. That was supposed to be the unspoken phrase that he was an informant of ours, but we weren't supposed to use the "I" word except amongst ourselves.

"He has to appear before the judge first, and the judge can release him on bail."

"When will he see the judge?"

"Tomorrow morning."

"He's been beat up pretty bad by the police, and he needs medical attention. Can he be sent to a hospital?"

"Yes, we can make arrangements for that." He looked over to the Duty NCO sitting at the desk. "Sergeant, can you arrange for the prisoner to be taken to the hospital?"

"Yes, sir," the sergeant replied.

"Thank you, captain," Paul added. We shuffled back out of the office, and Captain Simmons returned to his magazine.

There was no formal agreement between the Military Police and Tactical HUMINT Teams on how to handle such issues. It was all handled on a case-by-case basis, and the outcome depended upon the level of cooperation between the two entities. We could not demand that a certain prisoner be released any more than we could demand that any certain persons be detained and jailed. If the MPs didn't feel like there was enough evidence either way, they wouldn't do it, no matter what we told them.

But at least we could go back to his brother and now show that we had accomplished something by influencing his receipt of proper medical care. It was important that we be able to demonstrate that we had some sort of influence on things that the Coalition did. It was the only thing that gave us any credibility with the locals. Without any operational funds, we certainly weren't paying them anything, or offering much in the way of any other incentives. The cooperation of contacts and informants depended wholly on their generosity in sharing what information they had with us out of the goodness of their hearts.

We drove over to Camp Baker to meet with the MP Operations NCOIC to ask if he could influence the situation from his angle. It was apparent that we were not going to get any more cooperation from Captain Simmons. Based upon our history, he was not going to do anything for us that he absolutely didn't have to.

DAY 201: SUN 30 NOV 03

In talking with some of the agents from OGA, we learned that even their agency had no real focus in intelligence collection in Iraq. Everything was focused on predicting attacks against Coalition Forces. And like us, even when good intelligence was produced, no action was being taken.

Then the Salvadorans surprised us. A Salvadoran patrol went to the Kufa gas station and confiscated two AKs from *Mahdi* Army members. Shortly thereafter, a crowd of *Mahdi* Army supporters gathered around the patrol and chanted that they had more and better weapons inside the mosque. Then someone in the crowd called out their linguist by his name and tried to shame him for supporting the Coalition. Shortly thereafter, the Kufa police chief arrived, and told the Salvadoran officer in charge of the patrol that the two AKs were police weapons from his department that he had loaned to the *Mahdi* Army. This, of course, was strictly against regulations—and probably an outright lie—but since Ambassador Bremer had retained the sole authority to hire and fire any and all government officials in Baghdad, there was nothing anyone could do to the police chief about it. It was apparent to us that the police chief was working for Sadr now.

Sadr sent a representative to the provincial governor, and offered to assist the local governments with public works projects such as cleaning out sewers and such, as a public service project. The governor replied that as long as the *Mahdi* Army wasn't on the street with guns, then it would be OK. It was a real sly political move by Sadr to begin his infiltration of the local governments.

CHAPTER 5
W.M.D.

DAY 203: TUE 2 DEC 03

The fuel shortages continued across the country, raising tempers as well as gas prices on the black market. Processed gasoline, diesel, kerosene and propane was brought from the port of Basra via tanker trucks to the rest of the country. The truck drivers were paid by the Coalition. They were paid more to deliver to the more dangerous parts of the country such as Baghdad, Tikrit, Ramadi and Fallujah. Many of the drivers would divert their deliveries from more peaceful cities like Najaf so that they could earn a few more Dinars. On the other hand, there were some truck drivers that outright refused to drive unless they were paid more, no matter where they were going. It was a dangerous highway out there, and for some unknown reason, not all of the trucks were escorted by armed military escorts, but had to risk the trip on their own with no protection. When the Marines had been here, they had always provided security for fuel convoys, and there was hardly ever a problem. Now, for whatever reason, the MND was not always providing that same level of security. But then again, there were a lot of things that the MND was not doing that the Marines did.

Even after the fuel arrived at the stations, there was more corruption that exacerbated the fuel shortages. Some of the tanker truck drivers would only deliver part of their loads at the stations, and then would deliver the rest to black marketers for a higher price. The police at the stations who were supposed to maintain order were instead taking bribes to allow people to cut the long lines, or jacking up the prices at the pump and pocketing the difference. Some people had been waiting in line for up to *three days*.

When the Kufa mayor called on the police chief to take back control of the Kufa gas station from the *Mahdi* army, he ended up compromising instead. He gave *tacit approval* for the *Mahdi* army to control the gas station on behalf of the police. To top it all off, the Spanish had returned the two confiscated AKs to the *Mahdi* army—along with a written apology—in an effort to placate them. It would soon prove to have been too little too late.

DAY 204: WED 3 DEC 03

It had begun. At 0140, a handful of 60-millimeter mortar rounds were fired at Camp Animal, on the north side of Najaf, the camp where the Honduran battalion was based. There were no casualties and no damage. Everyone suspected that it was the *Mahdi* Army retaliating against the "Spaniards" for interfering with their control of the Kufa gas station. The *Mahdi* Army wasn't smart enough to differentiate between the Hondurans, Salvadorans, and the actual Spanish army; they were all lumped together and referred to simply as "the Spanish." This was the first real attack against the Coalition in Najaf.

During a visit with the Customs Police, we were happy to learn that they were receiving weapons, vehicles and communications equipment, vastly improving their capabilities. The interior ministry was issuing two RPG launchers for each outpost, and a host of PKM machine guns for heavy firepower. Now they would be able to take on terrorists and smugglers crossing the border. Vehicles were being transferred to them from the mayor's office, of all places. And they had received a large amount of funds for the purchase of radios for the outposts and for their vehicles as well. Surely, as time went by, things were improving for the Iraqis.

One thing Brigadier Hussein told me he did need for his department was concertina wire, so that he could secure his building from people just walking up to it from off the street. We went to Camp Baker and found a huge pile of wire and filled our truck beds with it and brought it back for them. It wasn't nearly enough, but it was a good start.

DAY 206: FRI 5 DEC 03

We drove past and checked both gas stations in Kufa. There was a second station across the river that we had been told had been taken over by the *Mahdi* Army as well, and we wanted to confirm that report. Sure enough, there were *Mahdi* Army at both stations, but there were no weapons visible. They probably had them hidden away nearby. The station across the river was closed, probably due to a lack of fuel to sell, but there were still a half dozen *Mahdi* Army sitting out front gabbing with each other. They jeered and made gestures at us as we drove past them.

DAY 209: MON 8 DEC 03

While reading the book *In the Company of Heroes* by CW4 (now retired) Michael Durant, the helicopter pilot that had been captured in Somalia in October 1993, Leyla came across a quote by retired General and now Secretary of State Colin Powell that reflected much of our dilemma here: "The commander in the field is always right, and the rear echelon is always wrong, unless proven otherwise." With the lack of action against Sadr and his *Mahdi* Army despite our numerous reports, it was the story of our team. I added the quote to my classified email signature block that night.

We drove around the Kufa riverfront that morning, looking for any unusual activity. There was a platoon of street sweepers out, cleaning up the streets and sidewalks. They eyed us carefully as we parked along the curb by the river and snapped some photos. We then drove to the end of the street where Saddam's small Kufa palace was. It had been earlier claimed by SCIRI, the same organization that was sponsored by Iran, and had teamed with the *Mahdi* Army in assassinating local former *Ba'ath* officials. SCIRI wasn't necessarily friendly with the Coalition, so it would be interesting to see how we would be greeted.

As we approached the open gate, there were a half dozen men sitting along the side of the road in plastic lawn chairs talking. We stopped and waited to see if any of them would approach us, but they all just continued to sit in their chairs and look at us. Mike and I climbed out and walked over to them, and asked if we could go take a look at the palace. They told us to go right ahead.

We drove through the open gates—there was no guard— and down the tree-lined street about a hundred meters to the palace. From what we could see, it was an empty shell. Like most other government buildings in Iraq, it had been stripped completely bare of everything. There were no doors or windows, outlets, light fixtures, plumbing—nothing. There was a construction crew working away on refurbishing the building, though. They were laying bricks and concrete blocks on the roof. They would have a long way to go before the building was finished. The construction crew was a bit surprised to see us, and smiled and said hello, but otherwise continued about their work as we wandered through the palace.

There was a grand stairway leading up to the front doors, which led into a diamond-shaped ballroom, with all glass walls looking out over the Euphrates river below. Of course, the glass was all missing now. On each side of the entryway were two towers, each containing a spiral staircase leading to the second floor, and then to the roof. The upstairs appeared to have what at one time would have been very large and fancy bedrooms with private baths, and even a tub. In the basement, there was a medium-sized swimming pool, now drained of course, and littered with garbage. During Saddam's reign, disco parties were held in the palace. Such decadence so near the holy places in Kufa and Najaf must have infuriated the local pious *Shi'ite* Muslims. Even during the Saddam regime, it was not uncommon for stores in the province selling alcohol to be bombed. They would simply toss in a grenade as they drove past.

We said goodbye to the crew and drove back out. There was an elderly man standing at the gate as we drove through. He closed the gate behind us. I guess they didn't want any more unexpected visitors.

DAY 211: WED 10 DEC 03

At about 0200, five mortar rounds were fired at Camp Baker, but all of them fell short, impacting in the farm fields to the northeast of the camp. Salvadoran patrols in the area from where the rounds had been fired from reported seeing a white pickup truck in the area. Military Police (MP) patrols were sent out.

At about 0400, the MP patrol that went through Kufa reported that they observed a white pickup truck parked in front of the Kufa mosque. Their Tactical Operations Center (TOC) instructed them to check the hood to see if it was warm. Since Coalition Forces were not permitted on mosque grounds, the patrol drove down the street to the Kufa police station to get a couple of Iraqi police.

While at the police station, the patrol saw a white pickup truck drive past the station, and they took pursuit. The truck continued down the main street, seemingly oblivious to the Humvee that was trying to catch up to them. There was no traffic at that time of the morning, so the truck continued at a high rate of speed.

The patrol radioed ahead, and the MPs at the Najaf police station blocked the street ahead with their Humvees. The truck approached the road block and came to a stop. The MPs, with guns drawn, yelled for the men to get out of the truck. Shaking with fear, they were ordered to the ground and zip-cuffed.

The truck was searched, but no weapons were found. Between them, the suspects had about 340,000 Dinars, or about 170 dollars. The suspects and the truck were transported to the nearby Najaf police station and incarcerated. Then the MPs called us and asked if we wanted them held or transported elsewhere. We instructed them to hold them.

Later that morning, we interviewed the MPs that had conducted the patrol and made the apprehension. We then went to the Najaf police station and thoroughly searched the truck personally for any clues or other evidence. There were four large plastic crates in the back of the truck. In the bottom of one of the crates was an old onion skin, indicating that the crates were used to haul around vegetables.

We then had the MPs take each suspect's photograph with our digital camera, and conduct a gunpowder residue test. If these men had actually been handling and firing mortars and mortar ammunition, there was sure to be gunpowder residue on their hands, face and clothing.

The test consisted of a large strip of clear tape, similar to scotch tape, only sturdier. The tape was pressed onto the suspect's hands, face and clothing. Then a small capsule containing some sort of chemical was poured onto the strip, and it was pressed between a white backing. If the chemical turned blue within three minutes, then the test indicated that there was gunpowder residue.

All four tests were negative. Had they washed the residue off in the meantime, and possibly even changed clothes at the mosque? Or were they perhaps not the attackers the MPs suspected them to be?

We studied their identification cards. Three of them lived in Abassiya, a town we knew to be a *Ba'ath* stronghold. The fourth lived in Al-Haria, a smaller village just the other side of Abassiya. Besides the cash, among their personal effects, one of them had a red military identification card, indicating that he had been labeled a deserter from the army at some point. Another had a scrap of notepad paper listing a number of different fruits and vegetables with their corresponding market prices.

We then went to the traffic police station and had them call their main office in Baghdad to run the plate. The vehicle information indicated that it was registered to the brother of one of the suspects.

We then went to visit one of our informants and had him look at the photographs, and to find out if had any information about the mortar attack. While the *Mahdi* Army were most likely responsible for the attack, there were also no positive identifications on any of the photographs.

After lunch, we went back to the Najaf police station to begin questioning the suspects individually. We separated into two teams, and interviewed two suspects each throughout the afternoon. Afterwards, we came together and compared notes.

It was unanimous. Every one of us felt that all four of them were telling the truth. There had been no signs of deception from any of the four during the interviews, and all four of their stories corroborated seamlessly. They all lived as neighbors in Al-Haria, worked in the market in Al-Haria, and every morning at about the same time, they met to ride to the market in Najaf, where the prices were best, and brought with them their cash from the prior day's sales to purchase the next fresh supply of fruits and vegetables to sell back at the market in Al-Haria. The amounts of money that each of them had were reasonable for such purposes, and was not unusual. As best as we could determine, these four men appeared to be victims of circumstance. If they were in fact *Mahdi* Army or terrorists, then they were very, very good at hiding it. But from what we had seen of the *Mahdi* Army, they were nothing more than a rabble of thieves and lowlifes that would most likely run at the first sound of gunfire. They certainly were not professionally trained fighters by any means.

At the meeting with the ranking officers of each battalion that evening, I spent about 20 minutes and told the entire story of our events during that day with the four men that had been apprehended, and concluded with our unanimous recommendation that they be released. The room went silent.

This was a prime example of how innocent people were rolled up by the military and shipped off to Abu Ghraib. We never did learn what happened to the four men.

DAY 213: FRI 12 DEC 03

When a Spanish patrol happened by during the Friday sermon, about 50 angry protesters blocked the street by stringing a steel cable in front of the Kufa gas station, and began yelling about the gas shortage and obscenities at the Spanish. The Spaniards escorted two of the ringleaders to Camp Baker to speak directly with First Lieutenant Chancosa, the Spanish civil affairs officer responsible for fuel in the city.

We drove through the Kufa market and past the Kufa mosque prior to the Friday noon sermon given by Sadr. Traffic was stop and go, as it usually was on Fridays, with a heavy load of vehicle and pedestrian traffic. While we were keeping a watchful eye, unbeknownst to us, three *Mahdi* Army members were following our trucks through the traffic on foot. We didn't know it at the time, but found out later they had hand grenades in their pockets, and intended to kill us.

Right in front of the mosque, the traffic unexpectedly cleared, and we accelerated into the breach and drove almost directly to the Kufa police station, where we parked and waited until the sermon was over. As we waited inside the guarded parking lot, the three assassins approached the gate guard and asked who we were. The police officer told them that we were American Soldiers. They went across the street to watch and wait, to see what we would do next. After a while, they realized that we were not going anywhere for a while, and they left.

DAY 215: SUN 14 DEC 03

Out in the desert north of Najaf lay a huge ammo dump comprised of 100 bunkers built by Yugoslavia for Saddam in the 1980s. Each bunker was the size of three basketball courts inside, and most were filled with every type of munition one could think of. There were literally thousands of tons of high explosives, mostly artillery shells. There were even artillery shells in calibers that Saddam didn't even have in his army. It was chaos.

Since there was no way to empty and inventory all of the bunkers, there may well have even been chemical or biological weapons in some of them. We wouldn't know until we emptied them all, and that would take several months. And there were a number of other ammo dumps just like this one strewn across Iraq.

A small group of American contractors was responsible for destroying all of it, and they slowly—and very carefully—gathered about a hundred tons per day and moved it to an empty quarter of the desert, and then ignited it in huge explosions that could be felt back in Najaf. These contractors were very concerned about looters, and asked for our help.

Escorted by four guards from the Ammo Supply Point (ASP), we went to visit a small village nearby. All four of the men were retired from U.S. military special operations. Three were former Special Forces, and the fourth was a former Navy SEAL named Mike who also doubled as a field medic.

We pulled off the asphalt road onto a dirt trail that led to a mud hut in the desert. As we parked, several Iraqi men came out of the hut and gathered around. Off in the distance were a number of other huts. Word passed quickly that there were visitors, and more men soon arrived.

The news of the day was the capture of Saddam Hussein. During the previous night, a Raider Force from Task Force 121 at Baghdad International Airport (BIAP) made up of Delta Force, SEALs and the 160th Special Operations Aviation Regiment (SOAR) flew north to Tikrit. There, they hooked up with the G-2 Intelligence Section personnel from 4th Infantry Division (4ID), who were running down a solid lead on the current location of Saddam. The Operation was dubbed "Red Dawn," named after the movie by the same title. About 600 troopers from the 4th Infantry Division had isolated the entire area around where Saddam was hiding to ensure that he would not slip away. MH-6 Little Birds from the 160th SOAR darted back and forth across the moonless black sky. Everyone was anticipating another brutal firefight like the one where Saddma's infamous sons, Uday and Qusay, had been killed.

After two earlier hideouts inside the cordon turned up dry, they came across a third one with a couple of men, a cook and his brother, living in a small hut. The Special Operators found a green footlocker filled with $750,000 in $100 bills. Then something caught the attention of one of the Operators, who noticed a thread of fabric protruding from the dirt, concealing a Styrofoam plug.

One D-Boy pulled the pin on a grenade while a second removed the plug from the ground, and the rest took up firing positions. Then unexpectedly, Saddam stood up out of the hole, thrust his hands in the air, and yelled in English, "I am Saddam Hussein, I am the president of Iraq, and I am willing to negotiate!"

The commando nearest him replied calmly, "President Bush sends his regards." Then several of the D-Boys yanked him from out of his hole and removed the loaded pistol from his belt. As they attempted to secure him, Saddam resisted, trying to shrug them off of him, and even spitting in one Soldier's face. He was forced to the ground, then bound with flex-cuffs and had a sandbag popped over his head, like any other prisoner. There was disagreement over how the large scratch appeared over Saddam's left eye. Some say that he was punched as he resisted and tried to reach for the pistol in his belt, but the official line was that he was unavoidably scratched while being removed from the tight confines of his hole.

A radio report was transmitted that the "Jackpot"—the code name used for Saddam—had been secured. Within minutes, he was whisked off to BIAP on a Little Bird. Not a single shot had been fired, and not a single Soldier had even been wounded in the entire operation.

After arriving at the prison compound at BIAP, Saddam was escorted through a silent gauntlet of TF121 soldiers on his way to his new detention facility. There, he was stripped naked and examined like any other prisoner. Then a few of his former aides that were already in custody were given the opportunity to see him from a distance, including his former Foreign Minister, Tariq Aziz, who also confirmed that it was indeed him. Then, four members of the new Iraqi Governing Council (IGC) were permitted to question him. When Saddam saw Adnan Pachachi, a *Sunni*, among the group, he asked him, "Why are you associating with these *Shi'ites*?"

We had only found out ourselves just prior to leaving the ASP, and yet a few minutes later, all of these people living in the middle of the desert were already aware of it before we had arrived. All of them were quite happy about the news. In Baghdad and other major cities around the country, the sky filled with celebratory gunfire.

To celebrate, we were invited to drink *chai*. Several blankets were brought out and laid in the sand between our trucks and the hut, and we gathered around and sat and chatted with them. There were about 20 men and boys gathered around.

Soon, *chai* was brought out and served. Since there weren't nearly enough tea glasses to go around, they were instantly recycled: as soon as one person finished, the same glass was refilled and offered to the next.

The villagers were tomato farmers that lived a very meager existence in the desert. The land was not even theirs, but was owned by others living in Najaf. They were allowed to live on the land for free and keep 25 percent of the profits from the sale of their crops. The tomato plants must have been a hardy strain to grow in the desert, and were protected from the dry heat from plastic sheeting over the plants.

Mike, the SEAL medic, asked if there were any medical issues. There was one man and another baby boy who were suffering from ear infections. He took out his medical kit and looked at each of them, and cleaned their ear canals for them. I'm not sure if it was very helpful medically, but at least they felt good about it.

The ASP team promised to bring a number of blankets to give to the villagers to help keep them warm at night. They had bought 50 blankets in a bundle at the market for just such occasions.

On the way back to our safe house complex, we passed through Revolutionary Circle, and watched a number of cars pass through waving green flags and honking their horns in celebration of Saddam's capture. Upon our arrival back at the safe house, we learned that our brigade had ordered a lock-down because of the news of Saddam's capture. We were not allowed to leave the compound until further notice, until the brigade could see what the national reaction to the news would be. It sounded overly cautious as usual—we should have been out on the streets celebrating with the rest of the country. The generals were too gun-shy that there were going to be reprisal attacks by *Ba'athists*.

It was our hope that Saddam's arrest would now take the wind out of the Former Regime Elements operating against the

Coalition, and the new Iraqi Governing Council would have their chance to run the country. We would have to wait and see. We learned later that *Shi'ite* gunmen had gone out later that night and killed several former *Ba'ath* officials that had undoubtedly been responsible for repressing and killing *Shi'ites* during Saddam's regime. Now that Saddam was in custody, the *Shi'ites* would become more confident.

DAY 216: MON 15 DEC 03

The lockdown continued. As General Sanchez's eyes and ears, he was deliberately choosing to make himself blind and deaf by keeping us locked down and off the streets. SF and OGA were still out and about, of course; it was only us that were not permitted to leave the compound and collect intelligence. The disparity made no sense.

The Hondurans called and said that they had an Iraqi walk in and demand that he would only talk to an American officer, but since we were locked down, we couldn't go talk to him, so we had to ask if he could meet us the next day. I sure hope whatever he had to tell us wasn't time-sensitive, and that he would actually come back. Potentially sensitive intelligence was missed all the time because of such ridiculous rules.

By 1500, Wendy at the OMT called and informed me that the lockdown had been lifted. I guess General Sanchez got tired of playing Helen Keller. We suited up and went into town to talk to people in the area of where the mortar attack had been launched.

People everywhere were happy and jovial that Saddam had finally been captured. Not only was it a massive psychological victory for the United States, but it served the same purpose to the people of Iraq as well. We pulled over by some farmers' fields. Paul, Joe and Moe walked off into the fields to talk to the farmers to find out if they had seen or heard anything the night of the attack. While they did that, Leyla and I stayed back and guarded the trucks.

Within minutes, we were mobbed by local boys and men wanting to meet Leyla. The crowd quickly grew to about 30, and Leyla and I kept backing up further towards the field. The crowd was very friendly, and we were not concerned so much for our safety, but Leyla was beginning to feel a bit claustrophobic with all of these people around us.

The other guys came back from the fields, and we moved on to talk to other people. We could not find anyone who had seen or heard anything of value to us about the mortar attack that night.

DAY 217: TUE 16 DEC 03

The morning started with a huge thunderstorm before sunrise. Storm clouds rolled in from the south spewing lightning and rolling thunder, then a sheet of rain blanketed the desert. By sunrise, blue sky peeked out here and there between the dark clouds.

We had once again been locked down. This time, it was by order of Colonel Pappas, our brigade commander at Abu Ghraib. Like our battalion commander, he also had never been to Najaf. His reason for locking us down was based on our report that the *Mahdi* Army had hunted us with grenades near the mosque during Friday prayers. He interpreted that to mean that they somehow knew who and where we were, and were coming to get us no matter what. In fact, it had been only a defensive maneuver on their part, and was only around the mosque, and was only during Friday prayers. And it was apparent by their actions that they did not know who we were.

Instead of doing the right thing and taking the *Mahdi* Army leaders into custody and locking them up for threatening Coalition Forces, the answer was to placate to their threats and blind the Coalition leadership. Intelligence reporting throughout the entire Najaf province dropped to zero until the lockdown was lifted. Additionally, all future appointments that we already had set with informants and contacts would be missed, and we would lose rapport with them. Some of them may even decide that we were not worth dealing with, and stop giving us information.

The leadership also failed to realize that we were not defenseless lambs. While we were a small element, we were armed and trained Soldiers, fully capable of defending ourselves. Despite this, though, we were instructed that we could not even go to Camp Baker for meals unless we were escorted by SF or MPs for extra security. Otherwise, we were instructed to eat the army bag-lunch MREs.

It was alarmist at an absurd level. The leadership was still reacting to the Clinton-era zero-defect mentality that had been ingrained during a decade of peace-keeping operations in the Balkans, where mission success was scored solely on there being no wounded or killed American Soldiers. Nothing else mattered. If a commander had made such a decision in a war zone before the Clinton era, he would have been relieved of command and court-martialed for cowardice. Now it was accepted as routine.

The enemy had already won. All they had to do was pose a threat, and the Coalition would run and hide. Our reaction only emboldened them even more, and served to de-legitimize the Coalition in the eyes of the populace, who now only saw us as impotent.

DAY 222: SUN 21 DEC 03

"CONTACT RIGHT!" We jumped out of the truck and took up our positions. Paul crouched behind the front tire, using the engine block as cover. Leyla crouched behind the rear tire. I exited from the passenger side and ran around the front of the truck, taking up a dual position next to Paul behind the engine.

We were conducting more React to Contact drills as part of our combat training to improve our security awareness. Just prior, we had taken each of our trucks out back to a flat open area of sand and practiced J-turns. It was a great maneuver to get out of a tight spot in a hurry. When confronted with a roadblock or other obstacle that you want to avoid to your front, everyone's first instinct is to turn around, which usually takes a number of turns and stops, especially for vehicles with a wide turning radius, or narrow streets.

The J-turn minimizes the number of actions, and when done smoothly, the vehicle never stops during the turn. The idea is to drive in reverse and then turn the wheel as fast as possible to the left while holding down the clutch. The momentum causes the front tires to break traction, and the front end of the vehicle swings around 180 degrees. As the vehicle is swinging around, the driver shifts from reverse to first gear, and then stomps the gas and pops the clutch as soon as the vehicle has a clear path. At first, it feels like you're out of control, but only because it's an unnatural feeling to drive without traction. But with practice, it becomes quite simple—and fun.

We learned from our drills that it's a lot faster—only about three seconds—to bail out of your own door and run around the truck than to crawl through the cab to exit the other side. It's tough to hit a moving target with only three seconds of exposure. Not impossible for an experienced marksman who's prepared for such a maneuver, but with Iraqis behind the trigger, it was a chance I was willing to take. Crawling through, especially with the parking brake and gear shift in the way, took much longer, and then you had to climb out of the vehicle head first—while holding your rifle. That was no easy task, took much longer than three seconds, and made you more of a stationary target.

After the drills, we practiced firing live from inside the vehicle, first from one side and then the other, just to get a feel of what it was like. The driver discovered the sensation of being hit in the back of the head by expended shells from the rear passenger's AK. I wanted to make sure everyone, including me, had that experience so that it wouldn't surprise them if it happened in a real situation.

DAY 223: MON 22 DEC 03

It was day seven of our restriction. We had lost contact with our informant network, and a number of our liaison contacts had by now discounted us. U.S. military intelligence reporting in our province had dropped off to nothing for a week now, and no one seemed to care. Considering that no one acted on our intelligence anyway, it just confirmed what we already suspected—no one truly cared about security in the Najaf province, as long as it wasn't all-out civil war. Sure, the Military Police were doing what they could with what meager resources they had, but they were stretched so thin, most citizens failed to notice them. They maintained their presence at the police stations and ran what vehicle patrols they could, but beyond that, they were strapped.

DAY 224: TUE 23 DEC 03

It was day eight of our command-imposed restriction. Most of our informants had by now most likely given up on us. The chief of the Customs police sent one of his majors to our gate to inform us that he had someone that had been waiting for us for four days now. This man supposedly knew the location of some buried uranium or other WMD stockpile. True or not, we would never know if we never took the opportunity to talk with him. I asked if they could bring the man to our gate, but they never returned that day.

Scott from the Ammo Supply Point (ASP) gave me a ride to the meeting that evening. The Military Police company had been notified that they were going to be transferring to a different city shortly after the New Year. That meant that the Iraqi Police would have even less oversight than they had now. On the way back, we drove through some sort of checkpoint on the main street in town. It was impossible to tell if the AK-armed men were police officers or not, as not a one of them was in uniform, and there was not a single police car in sight. They smiled and waved us right through with no hassles though. We didn't slow down enough to see who they might have been, as it might have ended up to our detriment.

DAY 225: WED 24 DEC 03 CHRISTMAS EVE

Captain Dave carbon-copied to me an email from CJTF-7, wondering why we hadn't submitted any reports in the last several days. His reply was that we had been locked down because people were out trying to kill us. I replied to all, and attempted to tactfully clarify that was not entirely accurate. Sure, someone had tried to kill us at one place in time, but no one was out actively hunting us down. Thus, the lockdown was arbitrary.

The Military Police had called informing us that they had a walk-in that wanted to share information with the Coalition. I called them back and informed them that we were locked down and would not be able to meet with the person. He was all theirs to deal with as they saw fit.

DAY 226: THU 25 DEC 03 CHRISTMAS

Christmas morning, I received a phone call from Lieutenant Elwell, the 716th MP Battalion Intelligence Officer. "We have two persons that you need to talk to. They're waiting for you at the 900th MP Company. They kept them there overnight. They say that they know the location of some rockets containing VX Nerve Agent."

"That's great, we'd love to talk to them, but we are not allowed to go anywhere unless we're escorted."

"We'll send over some MPs." I guess this time it was really serious. We donned our uniforms, and I shaved off my one week's passive-aggressive growth of beard. We loaded into our trucks and parked out by our front gate, waiting for the MPs.

The MPs arrived in two Humvees and escorted us over to Camp Baker. We went into their Tactical Operations Center (TOC) where the two men were waiting for us. Also in the TOC was Lieutenant Colonel Hayes, the new commander of the 706th MP Battalion. He had replaced Lieutenant Colonel Orlando after he had been Killed In Action in Karbala. He was a thin man with blond hair, and stood slightly taller than me. We shook hands and I introduced myself, and he was quite cordial and friendly. "Harry, I've been instructed by CJTF-7 to hold these guys for your team to debrief. Your guys have the training and experience to handle this and determine if they're credible or not. My MPs," he shrugged, "don't have your type of expertise. Is there anything that you need that we can provide for you?" I loved it when superior officers asked me that.

"All we need is a couple of rooms where we can talk to these men undisturbed."

"OK, I'll see what we can arrange."

"Thank you, sir."

He stepped away. "CAPTAIN SIMMONS!" he bellowed at the top of his lungs across the TOC. The captain ran up to him from across the room and went to parade rest in front of the colonel. "Yes, sir," he replied.

"Make sure that the THT has everything they need," he said in a low voice.

"Yes, sir."

Upon our arrival, we learned that there was a third man waiting down by one of the gates. The MPs had taken one of the two men with them to identify him and bring him also to the TOC. Leyla and Moe took the first man to another room and began debriefing him. Paul and Mike talked to one of the other men, who happened to be an attorney in town that they had met before.

Periodically throughout the debriefings, Colonel Hayes would pass by and ask, "What have you learned so far? Are they credible?"

"I don't know yet. They're still talking to them. I won't know anything until they're finished. I don't expect it to be more than another half hour at this point."

I knew and understood that he was as anxious as everyone else was to find out what these men had to tell us, but I wasn't about to go barging into the middle of their interviews just to ask them, "What have you learned so far? Are they credible?" Those poignant questions would have to wait until they were finished with the debriefings.

As it turned out, the first man was just a cousin of one of the other men, and didn't know anything. The attorney was just the messenger working to bring everyone together. The third man had been the one we needed to talk to. He had been a soldier assigned to a Republican Guard transportation unit, and during the war had driven another man along with 12 artillery rounds out to a place in the desert, where the other man buried the rounds. He claimed that he could bring the fourth man to us.

But there was one problem. Because we had been locked down, the attorney had tried but hadn't been able to bring them to us, so he had been forced to take them to the MPs. Now the MPs wanted to detain them as if they were prisoners, instead of treating them as volunteers. All this accomplished was to infuriate and frighten them. Here they had voluntarily come to the Coalition to share information about WMD, and had instead faced the possibility of getting locked up. It was no way to foster cooperation. I convinced the MPs to let them go so that they could bring the fourth man to us the following day. The MPs reported it up the chain that I had authorized the release of "their detainees."

After they had finished talking with the men, I sent the team to Christmas dinner before the dining facility closed. The menu posted outside stated that the Christmas meal was roast turkey, lobster tails, crab legs, roast beef, and all the trimmings. By the time I had arranged for the release of our guests, the chow hall had already stopped serving food. The only thing left was pumpkin and apple pie. I took a slice of each, and they were both delicious, although once again there was no whipped cream. When I met up again with the rest of the team and inquired as to how the meal was, unanimously they replied that it had been awful. There had been no turkey, lobster or crab legs, only roast beef, and even it was lousy. The "trimmings" were a huge disappointment as well. It would turn out to be the most memorable Christmas ever, only because it didn't feel like Christmas at all.

By now, the entire team was fed up with the whole lockdown. We didn't need a squad of MPs to baby sit us in our own city, so we blew them off and didn't even request an escort back to our compound, but drove into town on our own. We went to a new restaurant that had opened in town recently, and ordered take-out of all of our favorite dishes, and took them back to our safe house. After being deprived for so many days and a disappointing Christmas dinner, we had a craving for some good local food.

DAY 227: FRI 26 DEC 03

We went back to Camp Baker that afternoon, again blowing off the escort requirement. We had a job to do, and were going to do it whether we had a couple of extra guns along or not. The MPs had more important things to do than baby sit us, and we knew what the threat situation was, and how to take care of ourselves.

We had agreed to meet them at the gate instead of having them go inside the camp to the MPs again, and risk getting involuntarily detained. But after waiting an hour, they failed to show. We went into the camp to a local phone and called the attorney's office, the only number that we had. His secretary informed us that they had been gone all day and had not yet returned form wherever it was that they had gone.

It was already dark, and the gate was closed for the night,

so we figured that we would try again the following morning to reach them. We headed back to the safe house for the night.

Upon our arrival, we were told that our lockdown had been lifted! I immediately commenced planning our future operations and filled in our calendar with appointments of people that we needed to get caught up with. Then I went to pull guard duty.

It was 2200. Paul came out. "Captain Simmons just called, and said that the four men just arrived at his TOC (Tactical Operations Center). He wants you to call him back." Three of the men had left that morning to get the fourth man, only to find out that he had taken a job in the city of Bayji, north of Tikrit. They had spent the entire day driving there, locating him and convincing him to come back with them, and then driving back, where they went straight to the camp. After waiting for them ourselves and eventually giving up, we had left the camp four hours prior.

I went to the phone, dialed the number, and Sergeant Murphy answered. "Please inform them to meet us at the gate tomorrow morning at 0900, thanks." I hung up and went back to my guard post.

A few minutes later, the phone rang again, and I had to go back to the office. There was no escaping Captain Simmons.

"I'm under orders to detain these guys until they show us where they buried the weapons." I shook my head in disbelief. These were the kinds of things that ended up happening when other units entangled themselves in intelligence operations. Now our informants, who had of their own volition came at 2300 at night to talk with us, were being *arrested* by the MPs! That was going to go a long way towards promoting their co-operation in sharing information with us.

I called our OMT (Operations Management Team), and Captain Oliver answered the phone. Even before I could say anything beyond "hello," he said, "You need to get down there and debrief this guy right away. There are colonels in Baghdad that are very interested in what this man may have to tell us, and they are waiting for your report."

It was true, even at this hour. While the generals slept, there was a platoon of colonels to handle all of the finer details of everything that happened while they rested. In fact, each general had a specific "wake" list, specifying under what circumstances they were to be wakened and notified if certain events happened while they were sleeping.

We loaded up again and headed for Camp Baker. Leyla, Moe and I sat down with the now-famous fourth man and began debriefing him. Leyla started with a chronological history of the main events.

He appeared to be fit and in his mid-thirties, and had a military-style haircut, along with the obligatory and still-popular Saddam mustache. With Moe translating between them, Leyla asked him his name and rank, and what he had done in the Iraqi military.

"I am a warrant officer. I was in the Republican Guard, and my job was to inspect munitions."

"Okay, what do you have to share with us?"

"During the war, a small number of special artillery rounds had been brought to my base. My superior officers told me that they contained chemical weapons."

"What kind of chemical weapons?"

"VX nerve agent. We had orders to fire the rounds at Coalition Forces if they penetrated the second ring of the three defensive rings that had been established around Baghdad. However, my commander became very worried that the rounds may become damaged from all of the bombing by Coalition fighter aircraft, and that the VX may leak and kill a large number of innocent Iraqi people around our base. So he ordered me and the truck driver to take the rounds somewhere out into the desert and bury them—he didn't care where and he didn't want to know, and that no one but me should know where they were. My commander then told me that if the rounds were ever needed at a later time, I would be contacted."

"So what did you do next?"

"Once it got dark, the truck driver and I loaded the rounds onto his truck, and then we went out into the desert and buried them."

"Where did you bury them?" We pulled out a map of Iraq and unfolded it onto the table. He pointed out a location east of Baghdad. Unfortunately, it was well outside the Najaf province, and so was also outside our own area of operations. If we were to go there, we would need special permission, which I was confident that we would never get.

Tracing his route with his finger on the map, he continued. "We left the highway about here, and found a row of trenches. We drove to the last trench in the line, which was about a kilometer west of the highway, and laid the rounds there."

"How did you do it?"

"There were seven chemical rounds and five smoke rounds. I laid them in an alternating line nose to tail in the bottom of the trench. Then we filled in the trench with sand until it was level, and then I covered it over with some fig tree branches that were lying nearby."

"What were the dimensions of the trench?"

"It was about shoulder deep, about four meters long, and about a meter wide."

"What did you do next?"

"I waited a few months, and then tried to tell someone in the Coalition, but everywhere I would go, the soldiers at the gate would turn me away, thinking I was crazy or something. No one would believe me." As culturally ignorant as many of our Soldiers were, this was not surprising. The details he had been giving us, along with his rank and job, made his information quite credible so far. We continued to interview him.

"A few months later, I talked to my attorney friend about

it, and he had brought me here." I followed up with his personal data and specifics on the weapon, since that was my area of expertise.

"What caliber are the rounds?"

"They are 155 millimeters." That was credible, as there were large numbers of 155-millimeter artillery pieces in the Iraqi army.

"How long is the round?" He held his hands about a yard apart.

"What markings are there on the rounds?"

"There are two yellow bands around the shell itself, which identifies it as a chemical round."

"What type of artillery piece were they to be fired from?"

"A *Shiri*."

"A what? What's that?"

"It's what we call the artillery piece." While I was familiar with a wide variety of weapons, I had never heard of a *Shiri* before. So I tried to get more specifics from him.

"What is the military nomenclature of this artillery piece?"

"I don't know. We all just call it a *Shiri*." Now I was getting a bit leery that perhaps this guy was just jerking us around with a made-up story. How could a professional officer not know the nomenclature of his weapons? While this was always a possibility, his story was still quite plausible. After all, he was not an artillery officer, but a munitions inspector. There would be no reason to think that he would actually know what weapon system a particular munition would be for, especially something as common as a 155-millimeter artillery piece, of which there were dozens of varieties around the world.

"Where is the *Shiri* made?"

"It's made in Austria." Saddam had actually purchased hundreds of highly advanced G-30 artillery pieces from Austria during the Iran-Iraq war. It made sense that these super-guns would be assigned to Republican Guard units now. I learned later that the word *Shiri* was a nickname for the G-30 that the Iraqis used. The details of his story were still credible.

This was a fine example of the kinds of leads the Coalition was getting from Iraqis all across the country. The Iraq Survey Group (ISG), the organization created to find WMD in Iraq, claimed that they had no shortage of such leads. Additionally, there were still literally tens of millions of documents that were still in storage, waiting to be translated and examined, as well as considerable circumstantial evidence to be pursued. Iraq had been maintaining an infrastructure to research better methods to weaponize biological munitions, just waiting for the UN inspection teams to leave.

He was willing to show us where the rounds were buried, but he was also interested in any reward that may be available from the Coalition. There may very well have been a reward program, but I didn't have any information about that.

When we had finished talking, I tried to call the OMT for guidance and assistance in getting these men released. The MPs had already put out four cots in anticipation of keeping them all in custody, and they were quite nervous about not becoming Coalition prisoners. The OMT's phone line was out, so I was left with no choice but to go through the MPs and try to convince them on my own to release them. I felt pretty sure that I would lose, especially without any clout from the OMT to back me up. Our new friends were getting really nervous, pacing back and forth, and muttering among themselves.

I called Colonel Hayes at Camp Babylon. "I'm being ordered by colonels at CJTF-7 C2 (intelligence) to keep all of these men in custody, and it's going to take more than your operations officer calling me to get them released," Hayes told me.

"Sir, these men are informants, not prisoners. They came in on their own to volunteer the information that they gave us. There is no reason to think that they will not return. I recommend that these men be released on their own recognizance."

"I'll pass your recommendation on to the C2, and it would ultimately be their decision."

Knowing that some obscure staff officer in some faraway location with no connection to events on the ground would be the one to decide their fate did not make me confident. They didn't seem to understand that these were not detainees, but willing and—so far—cooperative informants. If they were arrested and then decided to no longer cooperate, what were they going to do to them to find the location of the buried weapons of mass destruction? Waterboard them until they agreed to show us? This type of interference in intelligence operations by the MPs and other non-intelligence entities continued to be a problem in Iraq.

After about a half hour of phone calls back and forth, Colonel Hayes called one last time. "I explained your recommendation, and the colonel I talked to agreed with you. They are free to go."

I was stunned, hesitating a few seconds to let the answer sink in before thanking him and hanging up.

Naturally, they were quite happy, shaking my hand vigorously and smiling and thanking me. We walked them out to the gate so they could get to their car. The driver carried a case of bottled water he had grabbed out of the hallway of the MP building. We agreed to meet them again mid-morning. It was already 0130.

We drove home and fell into our cots. As I lay there, too excited to sleep, I realized that we had forgotten to write and submit a spot report on the warrant officer's willingness to show us the place where the warheads were buried. I decided to write it first thing after I woke up. The colonels would just have to wait a while until I was a bit more coherent.

DAY 228: SAT 27 DEC 03

My alarm went off way too early that morning. I stumbled over to the office and typed up the spot report and sent it out.

The phone line to the OMT was still down, and we had no point of contact to hand these guys off to, to take them to the spot where the VX-filled artillery rounds had been buried. I sent another email to the OMT explaining that our plan was to simply bring them with us to the OMT, and then determine from there what to do with them. We were only going to bring the munitions inspector and the truck driver, and thank the attorney and the cousin for their assistance. Since they didn't have direct knowledge, they didn't need to come along.

We waited at the meeting place for them, and again they failed to show. Moe went into the camp to call them on the local phone. He returned a while later. "They said that they are not coming in until they have three guarantees. First, they want a guarantee that they won't be arrested any more. Second, they want assurances that they will be safe, and that their cooperation with us will be kept confidential. And third, they want confirmation about any reward program, specifically about how much money they will receive and when they would receive it."

This was just great. I had put my reputation on the line to get these guys sprung so that they would cooperate with us, and now they weren't coming in. The MPs had once again worked against us in what could potentially have been one of the most significant events of the war.

Items one and two were no problem: all we had to do was keep them away from the MPs. But I still had no information on reward programs. The ISG had apparently done a lousy job of advertising any of their reward programs—if they did in fact exist—since none of the THTs knew about them. Who did they think would be the primary source of getting the ISG this information? I had seen no flyers, nor received any emails.

We decided to go to Camp Babylon without them. We needed to pick up Sami, who was back from his R&R leave, and while we were there, perhaps we could get more specific information about rewards, and who to hand them off to.

While we were there, we ate lunch, and Leyla and I wrote up a detailed report of everything that the Iraqi weapons inspector had told us. Just about then, "Captains Courageous"—Oliver and Dave—came strolling in. They had just returned from a run to Karbala where they had dropped off another Soldier returning from leave.

We didn't know it yet, but it was at about this time that the Coalition bases in Karbala were under attack. The captains had left just in time. Both Coalition camps were attacked with a combination of four different truck and car bombs, and the provincial governor's office was mortared. Three of the four car bombers were shot and killed before reaching their destinations, which greatly reduced the number of casualties. The fourth car bomb detonated in front of the provincial governor's office.

We picked up Sami and headed back to Najaf. We called the four men to give them an update, basically that we were still waiting for more information to share with them, since no one had any immediate information about any reward program, even at our headquarters. The secretary informed us that they had left, and she was not sure where they had gone to or when they would return.

This was not really turning out well. Now the Iraqis that I had tried so hard to earn their cooperation with had fled. I could see now that if we were unsuccessful in getting them back, I would probably be held responsible by some colonel somewhere for "letting them go" when we had the opportunity to take them into custody. I was not too worried about it, though.

The munitions inspector had told us that he needed to get back to his job, and it was unfair to him that we, the Coalition, had left him hanging with no information for so many days. I still did not have any information about any reward program, despite trying all day. The onus was still on us. Once we had the information, then we would attempt to re-contact him. And we could use the attorney as the messenger, since he lived right here in town. We would cross that bridge when we got to it.

As for now, the Coalition had let these men down, despite their best efforts to assist us—on more than one occasion. I was now the one that would have to repair all the damage that had been previously done by the insensitive and overzealous MPs, and see if we could provide some actual chemical weapons for President Bush to show to the world, thus proving that he had been right all along. I was convinced that the artillery rounds were there, even though I also knew that I would never see them personally, unless they were put on the news.

At the meeting that evening, I was immediately ambushed by Captain Simmons, who wanted to know if we were still in contact with the men. He had to report to his battalion—as if the situation had anything to do with them. I assured him that we had the situation in hand, and didn't mention that the men were gone. It was not an MP matter anyway.

As it turned out, the three men had gone to Baghdad and reported their information to an investigative team from the Iraqi National Congress (INC), led by Ahmed Chalabi, the same person that was later suspected of passing to Iranian intelligence officers that our own National Security Agency (NSA) had cracked their encoded communications and was reading their mail. The Pentagon discovered this when they intercepted an encrypted message from an Iranian intelligence officer informing his superiors of the leak in their communications—using the same code.

I was shocked to learn from a Master Sergeant from the Utah National Guard, the case officer at the Iraq Survey Group (ISG) that was assigned to our case, that the INC was also collecting intelligence from Iraqis on possible WMD—independent of the ISG. The INC was being paid $335,000 a month by the Defense Intelligence Agency (DIA) as part of an Information Collection Program (ICP) run by the INC to gather intelligence on the former regime. Since the beginning of the occupation, the INC had been working closely with the DIA and the U.S. military in Baghdad, feeding intelligence on the whereabouts of top *Ba'athists* and the movements of insurgent cells. At least two DIA agents were attached to the ICP to coordinate the flow of any intelligence collected by the INC agent networks. The INC had undoubtedly been using the funds that we were paying them to collect WMD intelligence as well, offering their own rewards for such information. They were trying desperately to gain some credibility since they also had loudly supported the position that Saddam had WMD. If they could find some and hold it up to the world, Chalabi would have greater legitimacy and support for his claim to be anointed as Iraq's next president.

I learned later from the Master Sergeant that he had been assigned to the ISG to work for an all-female group of CIA analysts that supposedly specialized in WMD that was known within the CIA as "The Sisterhood." The military members of the ISG nicknamed them the "Bio Chicks." The Bio Chicks were led by an analyst from the CIA who was entrusted to find WMD, but was utterly contemptuous of the military in general, and their silly macho intelligence system in particular. She purged all military personnel off the team and filled their places with CIA personnel. She gathered around her various university professors who considered themselves ace spies and genius scientists, and they got caught up in the super-sleuth world of the CIA. They actually were genius scientists, and supposedly did want to find WMD—but only in their own way. Feminism, anti-military attitudes, and CIA arrogance all seemed to play a part. It wasn't a pretty picture.

When I explained to the Master Sergeant the difficulty I had in never finding any information about the ISG's WMD information reward program, he said that there never really was one. He explained that the ISG analysts and investigators were burned many times by false leads and by Iraqis trying to scam reward money out of them for false information about Iraqi WMD. They were also burned out from running to and fro all over Iraq and not finding the coveted "mother lode" of chemical weapons or bio labs that they had come to expect. It eventually reached the point where the Bio Chicks simply dismissed all WMD intelligence brought to their attention by the military members of the ISG. The result was that nothing was done on future leads like ours.

The chemical artillery rounds were never pursued. No one from the Coalition ever went to the location and dig up the spot to determine if anything had actually been buried there. Who knows what would have happened if we had been listened to a little more?

It is widely believed in liberal circles that Bush lied about the existence of WMD in Iraq in order to persuade the nation to support an invasion. Lieutenant General Michael DeLong (USMC, retired) served as General Tommy Franks' second in command. DeLong published in his own memoir, "Inside CENTCOM: The Unvarnished Truth About the Wars in Afghanistan and Iraq," that he was ultimately convinced of the existence of Iraqi WMD based upon multiple intelligence reports from multiple nations, and that much of it had been smuggled into Syria just prior to the war, as well as some to Lebanon and even Iran. Just two days before the war started, there were multiple corroborating reports of huge caravans of trucks and vans crossing into Syria, carrying a number of the Top 55 Most Wanted.

Reports emerged later of a war between the CIA and the White House, speculation that perhaps the CIA had attempted to cover up any evidence of WMD in Iraq to get back at the Bush administration for blaming them for embarrassing them in front of the United Nations. The CIA supposedly leaked flaws into the intelligence reports to make the White House lose credibility. In response, Rumsfeld and Vice President Cheney created their own intelligence estimates because they were unhappy with the CIA's. When it looked as if there would not be any substantial amounts of WMD found in Iraq, Bush decided that CIA Director Tenet would be the scapegoat. On July 11, 2003, Bush sold Tenet down the Potomac and "accepted" his resignation. Tenet knew that he was being asked to resign so that Bush could be re-elected.

There were other credible reports of Russian Spetsnaz units cleaning out all of the WMD in Iraq and dumping it in the deepest recesses of the Indian Ocean or re-locating it to Syria, just weeks prior to the U.S. invasion. The following excerpt is from an article by national security journalist and best-selling author Kenneth R. Timmerman published on February 19, 2006:

> In December 2002, former Russian intelligence chief Yevgeni Primakov, a KGB general with long-standing ties to Saddam, came to Iraq and stayed until just before the U.S.-led invasion in March 2003. Primakov supervised the execution of long-standing secret agreements, signed between Iraqi intelligence and the Russian GRU (military intelligence), that provided for clean-up operations to be conducted by Russian and Iraqi military personnel to remove WMDs, production materials and technical documentation from Iraq, so the regime could announce that Iraq was "WMD free." This type of GRU operation, known as "Sarandar," or "emergency exit," has long been familiar to U.S. intelligence officials from Soviet-bloc defectors as standard GRU practice;
>
> In addition to the truck convoys, which carried Iraqi WMD to Syria and Lebanon in February and March 2003, two Russian ships set sail from the (Iraqi) port of Umm Qasr headed for the Indian Ocean, where they "deep-sixed" additional stockpiles of Iraqi WMD from flooded bunkers in southern Iraq that were later discovered by U.S. military intelligence personnel. The Russian "clean-up" operation was entrusted to a combination of GRU and Spetsnaz

troops and Russian military and civilian personnel in Iraq under the command of two experienced ex-Soviet generals, Colonel-General Vladislav Achatov and Colonel-General Igor Maltsev, both retired and posing as civilian commercial consultants. The two Russian generals had visited Baghdad no fewer than 20 times in the preceding five to six years. U.S. intelligence knew the identity and strength of the various Spetsnaz units, their dates of entry and exit in Iraq, and the fact that the effort to clean up Iraq's WMD stockpiles began with a planning conference in Baku from which they flew to Baghdad. The Baku conference, chaired by Russian Minister of Emergency Situations Sergei Shoigu, laid out the plans for the Sarandar clean-up effort so that Shoigu could leave after the keynote speech for Baghdad to orchestrate the planning for the disposal of the WMD. The evacuation of Saddam's WMD to Syria and Lebanon was an entirely controlled Russian GRU operation. It was the brainchild of General Yevgenuy Primakov. With Iran moving faster than anyone thought in its nuclear programs, the Bush administration needed the Russians, the Chinese and the French, and was not interested in information that would make them look bad. The goal of the clean-up was to erase all trace of Russian involvement in Saddam's WMD programs, and was a masterpiece of military camouflage and deception.

There were multiple reports of WMD being buried all over the country. And let's not forget that if Saddam really didn't have anything to hide, he wouldn't have played cat and mouse with UNSCOM for 12 years, as it ultimately would have been in his best interest to let them look anywhere they wanted for something that supposedly never existed. Saddam's WMDs are still out there, and someday their existence will be made known to the world—the hard way.

As I was pulling a shift of guard duty, the phone rang.

Oliver told me, "I just got a sketchy report of a hostage crisis in your town, something involving the governor, the chief of police and Sadr. I want you to go into town and see what you can shake up—right now."

Leyla volunteered to stay back and man the guard post while the rest of us suited up into our battle rattle and headed into town. It was already 2200. We visited a couple of Iraqi police stations and talked to the officers, then stayed for a bit to monitor the situation.

Sadr had passed through a Traffic Control Point (TCP) run by Iraqi police in the city that morning. The Iraqi policemen were supposedly a bit rude to him, and Sadr had been quite unhappy about it. Later that afternoon, two busloads of armed *Mahdi* Army surround the checkpoint. Seven officers ran for their lives, while four were captured and severely beaten with rifle butts. Then they were dragged into Sadr's secret court, where the governor and police chief were now attempting to negotiate for their release. Since the court was next to the Imam Ali shrine, we were not permitted to go near it. The Coalition's self-imposed restrictions had provided a sanctuary for our enemies to operate against us and the rest of the population.

I called in a verbal report, and then went to man the guard post for my three hours of guard duty from midnight until 0300. A dense fog rolled in from the west, reducing visibility to about 20 feet, and sucking away any remaining heat. It was a bone-chilling cold, the kind one would hardly expect in the Iraqi desert.

DAY 229: SUN 28 DEC 03

Thousands of Sadr's followers marched through the streets this morning in remembrance of the 1999 anniversary of the assassination of Sadr's father, Mohammed Sadiq, by Saddam's feared *Mukhabarat*. To the beat of drums, men flogged themselves with chains and women beat their chests. The demonstration passed without violence, although many residences feared that it would make them targets like what had happened the day before in Karbala. Sadr himself was absent from the ceremonies. *Mahdi* Army thugs dressed in black patrolled the streets alongside the demonstrators, openly brandishing their AK-47s, attempting to portray themselves as visible deterrents to any threats. American forces were nowhere to be seen, and the Iraqi police and Spanish ignored them, which by default gave control of the streets to these thugs.

Some of our informants were telling us that Sadr's *Mahdi* Army had been the ones that had attacked Karbala. Supposedly, they had built the bombs inside the mosque in their sanctuary in Kufa, and they were planning attacks against Coalition camps in Najaf next. Had we not been locked down, it's possible that we would have known about the attacks in Karbala before hand, and possibly even been able to prevent them. At the same time, there were reports that five suspects had been arrested in Karbala.

Our local guards reported having seen a number of vehicles on a repeated basis that would park in certain places around our safe house compound at certain times of the day, observing our routines. The SF team was going to try to ambush some of them tomorrow.

CHAPTER 6
NEW YEAR'S WEDDING

DAY 233: THU 1 JAN 04

At the Kufa gas station next to city hall, and across the street from the Kufa mosque, the gas line stretched for several blocks. The local Iraqi police that were there to supposedly maintain order were instead accepting bribes from some motorists to allow them to jump the line. This angered the rest of the people so bad that about 500 of them ran off the police and took over the station for themselves.

The following day, the *Mahdi* Army once again took control of the station. The Coalition stood by and did nothing about it.

DAY 237: MON 5 JAN 04

A group of about 15 or so men was walking along the north perimeter fence at about 0300. The guards spotted them in the perimeter lights, got nervous about their size and proximity, and opened fire on them. Someone from the group fired back, and then all hell broke loose.

At that point, all of the guards that had a line of fire began shooting at the group. Our Tenth Mountain boys contacted the SF, who then took up positions on the rooftops. By then, the group had scattered. I, along with everyone else on my team, had slept through the entire incident.

Sami had been real sick the last couple of days. Joe and Paul were home on leave. We had taken in a new linguist, Ali, on loan to us from the Diwaniyah team, as a stopgap until a new linguist was assigned to us. I had to fire Mike and Moe for suspicion of stealing weapons and ammunition, for being uncooperative in the conduct of their translation duties, and for threatening physical violence against one of the other team members. As they were packing up, Mike tried to steal one of the Thuraya satellite phones that had been loaned to us by the OGA. After we dropped them off at Camp Baker, I discovered that Moe had kept a brand-new Dragunov SVD sniper rifle hidden under his cot that none of us had known about, and was too long for him to take with him without being blatantly obvious.

And to think that these were American citizens with security clearances. We were supposed to be able to trust these guys. It was a great disappointment, and an eye-opener to me. Looking back on their many odd behaviors and other little things that had turned up missing here and there over the last few months, it made me feel violated. It was a bitter lesson learned.

It seems that CJTF-7 finally took an interest in our reporting, and finally decided to take action against the Sheikh that tried to kill us. It was reported that he had also been the leader of the car bomb attacks in Karbala, which is probably what really prompted the sudden interest. Even though we now had Ali and were up to four people again, Sami was suffering with suspected Salmonella poisoning. He remained restricted to quarters for two days before he was well enough to go out. It was during this time that we were instructed to go into town and collect targeting data on the Sheikh.

A major from CJTF-7 went to our headquarters at Camp

Babylon. He had been tasked with assembling a target folder on Sadr. Captain Oliver called, ordering us to make contact with any informants that we had that could provide such intelligence. They would just have to wait.

I did not feel the least bit guilty about not being able to conduct our mission because we were short handed. If anything, it infuriated me. Two of my Soldiers were home on their R&R leave, and after all that we had been through, we earned it. Because of the tight window available for us to take our leaves, our command tried to get as many Soldiers home as possible. If the Army hadn't put us on hold from taking leave for three months, we would not have been crunched for time like this. So it was the Army's fault in the first place for poorly resourcing and planning this entire operation. Our Soldiers were going to take their leave, even if it crippled the mission. And at this point, I was so angry at the callous disregard for our mission, I didn't give a damn. Apparently, our command felt likewise, or they wouldn't have let everyone take leave at the same time.

Some *Ba'athists* had buried a cache of weapons in the courtyard directly behind one of the local courthouses before the war. Among the standard fare of AKs, RPGs and ammo, it also supposedly contained some SA-7 shoulder-fired surface-to-air-missiles. We would have to get it dug up to find out for sure, and to prevent anyone else from getting them.

DAY 240: THU 8 JAN 04

One of the Iraqi guards from our compound was getting married to his first wife this evening, and he had invited us to the wedding celebration. While the actual ceremony had taken place the day prior, this was the festive reception-style celebration that traditionally took place the day after the wedding. It involved all of the friends and relatives—as well as everyone in the neighborhood—going to the groom's parents' home. The groom is taken on a celebratory drive through town, with a caravan of cars in tow. Young men would hang out the windows, whooping and yelling, everyone honking their horns. The groom's car was decorated with ribbons and flowers. In most cases, the bride also rode along, but not always, depending on how conservative the families were. If they were against having the bride being seen in public, then she would not go.

Leyla wore a dress she bought, and donned her *abaya* and *hejab* over it. Everyone in the compound wanted their photo taken with her dressed like that. The guard's brother was supposed to meet us at the gate, but there was a misunderstanding about which gate, and after waiting for an hour, we had missed each other. Since the wedding was just down the road, we decided to see if we could find it on our own.

We came right to the wedding. The crowd of people gave it away. It looked as if the entire village had turned out. The dirt street was filled with men and boys of all ages. Naturally, there were no women on the street. They were already inside the house partying. The groom had already left on his victory ride. Someone asked us if wanted to join the convoy. We accepted, and the brother jumped in to show us the way.

We took off past the cement factory, then went through the Kufa market, and down by the Euphrates river. I donned my Arab head scarf, and with Leyla in her *abaya*, the people in the marketplace didn't even notice that we were Americans. Along the river, we passed by about a dozen other wedding celebrations doing the same thing. There were dozens of vehicles in each party, all honking their horns, with men hanging precariously out the windows with video cameras filming the event. Everyone was whooping and waving. One party was parked on the curb, and the men were carrying the groom around on their shoulders, and everyone was dancing.

We passed each party, looking for ours, but never found it. On the way back, we passed through another wedding party. The traffic was so congested that one of the cars rear-ended another, but they were all so caught up in the celebration, everyone just kept on driving as if nothing had happened. Out on the cement factory road, we were passed by yet another wedding party that had teen age boys dancing on the roof of a bus as it careened down the road at over 40 miles per hour. One tap of the brakes, and they would have all gone flying through the air to their deaths.

We arrived back at the groom's neighborhood, and their own convoy had just returned. As I drove slowly down the darkened street, I passed a man walking in the opposite direction with an AK rifle. There was celebratory firing taking place, with a number of people standing in the streets and shooting a variety of AKs and pistols into the air.

We got out of the truck, and Leyla was immediately ushered away to the adjoining house where the women were gathered. They were in the process of conducting their own celebration, away from the men. Leyla reported later that once inside, *abayas* were removed, and all of the women were ornately dressed and wearing make-up. Loud music was playing, and everyone was dancing. She felt a little uncomfortable, as her presence as the token American was taking some of the attention away from the bride. The bride didn't look entirely happy, which was understandable, since it was an arranged marriage, and she probably hardly knew the groom. But it was their custom, as it had been for thousands of years. The idea was that bride and groom would develop a relationship and grow together and learn to love one another. For most westerners, it was a difficult concept to grasp. But then again, the divorce rate in the east was lower than in the west as well, which could also be read both ways.

The crowd called on Ali and me to fire our weapons in honor of the bride and groom. Not to do so would have been considered an insult, not a good position to be in as an honored wedding guest. On the other hand, celebratory fire was frowned upon and highly discouraged by the Coalition, who tried everything they could think of to discourage the citizenry from participating in it. The gesture was of course useless, as every Thursday, the skies lit up with red tracers and the sounds of gunfire, but only slightly more so than the other nights of the week. The Coalition even used the reason that celebratory fire was dangerous—eight people had been killed in Tikrit from the celebratory fire that resulted from Saddam's capture—but it was to no avail. The tradition went back as far as firearms had existed—hundreds of years—and pleas from a Coalition that had been in place for only a few months, and was only going to be around for only a few more, were not about to change such traditions.

Ali pulled out his pistol and started firing into the air. I flipped my AK's selector lever to auto, elevated the barrel at a 45-degree angle for maximum range, pointed it southward into the open desert beyond the village, and let loose with a deafening five-round burst. Having never fired the AK without ear plugs, I hadn't realized how loud it was. My ears started ringing immediately.

Someone in the crowd, shouted out, "Again!" I fired off another five-round burst. "Again!" came from the crowd. I tapped off a third burst.

"Again!" This guy seemed insistent that I empty the magazine, but then others in the crowd began murmuring to him to back off, and I had already fired enough. I flipped the lever back over to safe, and we were ushered into a meeting room. We removed our footwear, and sat on some thick rugs at the far end of the rectangular room.

Ali and I were a bit surprised that there was hardly anyone else in the room. Where were all the other guests? Ali inquired, and was told that because we were considered "special" guests, we were being given our own room to celebrate, separate from the rest of the party. Ali asked if we could join the rest of the group, as it was going to be quite a boring evening if we were going to be kept to ourselves.

We were escorted next door, where the walls of the room

were lined with the other wedding guests. There were about 20 Iraqi men dressed in traditional tribal wear: black and white checkered scarves with the black rope retainers, and brown robes worn over either western style business suits or formal *dishdashahs*.

As we entered the room, everyone stood—as was tradition. Ali and I stepped from man to man, going around the room, and greeting them in traditional Arab style: a handshake, and verbal greeting of "*Salaam alaykim* (peace be unto you)," accompanied by the traditional kissing of each cheek, depending if the other person felt close enough to you or not. About half of the men kissed me, a good sign that I was accepted by them.

We were directed to the place of honor at the end of the room, where I sat between the two oldest men in the room, resting my AK in the corner. Seniority and respect within tribes were mainly determined by age. Typically, the oldest man in any village was the tribal elder. Everyone in the room was looking at me, and more of the younger people crowded into the far end of the room at the doorway to look as well. There were even kids at the iron-barred window staring in at me. It was as if I was the first American any of them had ever seen up close, which was probably accurate. I just continued to smile respectfully, trying not to look uncomfortable.

One of the younger men sitting a few men down from me on my right made a statement in Arabic, as none of them, other than Ali, spoke any English. Ali translated, "The Americans were responsible for bringing Saddam to power, and now they are responsible for removing him from power."

Another of the elders on the other side of the room admonished him to change the subject, that this was a wedding celebration, and was not the place to discuss politics. Perhaps it had been the first man's way of showing his disapproval of my presence at the celebration. But it didn't matter, as we had been invited by the groom.

There was more weapon firing outside. It was so loud, it sounded like it was right outside the doorway. Some of them elaborated that there were a couple other weddings in the village that night, and the firing was celebratory for those occasions. My ears were still ringing from when I had fired my own AK earlier.

The dinner was brought in. First came a bowl of sweet rice topped with a half chicken. Then came a bowl of lentil soup, followed by flat bread. Once everyone had been served, we dug in. As a gesture of good hosting, the elder to my left on the other side of Ali ripped off strips of meat from his chicken and started putting it in my bowl. Ali asked him in Arabic to please stop, and then told me in English, "We don't know when the last time he's washed his hands." I took my chances and ate the chicken anyway, so as not to offend his gesture of generosity.

A group of young men and boys at the far end of the room gestured for me to take their photo. I took out my camera and snapped a picture of them. At that point, all of the other elders also asked that I take their photo. Since it was a digital camera, and didn't use any film, I happily obliged them, showing them the screen on the back of the camera after each shot, so they could see themselves.

After a while, the groom came in and told us that it was almost time for him to go in and take the bride. In traditional Arab custom, the couple is married the first day, but do not consummate the marriage until the following evening, which was the purpose of this celebration. Everyone filtered outside into the street. We gathered around the groom, and everyone started clapping their hands in unison and chanting something in Arabic that I didn't understand. The group escorted the groom to the doorway of the room where the women were celebrating with the bride. The men were not allowed further beyond that point, so we never got to see any of the other women, or even the bride for that matter. At that point, the groom entered the room, taking the bride by the hand, and went together into an adjoining bedroom. The women cheered as well as the groom entered the room and took the bride. The doors were closed, and out in the street the celebratory fire commenced once again. The inner courtyard erupted in fire from numerous pistols all around me. I covered my ears to keep from going further deaf. As we filtered out of the courtyard, one of the young teen-age boys came up to me and showed me his browning Hi-Power automatic pistol. Unfortunately, he was not very safety conscious, and he was inadvertently pointing it at me while showing it. I reached out and gently pushed the barrel away from me off to the side. Everyone standing around us was watching, and began laughing. Weapons safety was certainly not an Arab virtue. No harm was intended though, so I did not take offense. It had been an ignorant, yet innocent, mistake.

At that point, the new wedding couple was afforded privacy to consummate the marriage. Then the groom was expected to come back outside with the bed sheets in hand and show them to the crowd. The sheets were to be stained with the blood of the bride's virginity, and were displayed as a badge of honor for the bride's family. In the Arab culture, it was considered a great disgrace to the family to lose one's virginity outside of marriage, and often resulted in "honor" killings of young women by relatives to "restore" the family's honor. It was quite common for the bed sheets to be hung on public display from the tops of the house the following day for the entire village to see.

I didn't see the advertisement of the bed sheets. Leyla came out, and as the consummation ended, she shattered another glass ceiling in Iraq. Traditionally, women were not permitted to fire weapons in Arab culture, especially celebratory fire at a wedding. But since Leyla was American, she was given the opportunity, if she so chose to. Surrounded by a throng of about a hundred villagers, she took her AK and, still wearing her *abaya*, popped off a few rounds into the air. Everyone cheered.

Since we had been separated throughout the wedding celebration, Leyla's experience had been a bit different than mine. With her permission, I have included here a transcript of a letter that she wrote about her part of the adventure:

> *Dear Family and Friends,*
>
> *We finally have a concrete date as to when we are finally coming home, 27 March! That will make 14 months since I've slept in my own bed.*
>
> *It has finally gotten to the point here where it feels less and less like work. I can honestly say that I've grown accustomed to if not fond of this country and some of its peoples. A couple weeks ago I was invited to the wedding of one of our local Iraqi guards. He was to marry his first wife out of four that the Koran allows a Muslim man to wed.*
>
> *I was one of two Americans to attend. I had no idea what to expect in an Islamic wedding, but knew it was an opportunity of a lifetime. I dressed in the traditional* hejab, *which is the head-scarf and black robe. Women are absolutely forbidden to be seen by men other than their husband in anything but this outfit.*
>
> *The wedding started as a convoy of dozens of cars at the beauty salon to pick up the bride. We drove all over town to the religious sites honking our horns. Upon arrival at the home of the groom's parents, I was whisked away alone into a house separated from the men, and my American companion and translator. I have picked up a little Arabic along the way, but hardly enough to carry a conversation. I foresaw a night of a lot of hand gesturing.*
>
> *By tradition the men have their own celebration, and the women and children have theirs. I entered a small two-room home filled beyond capacity. I was greeted warmly with hugs and kisses from the women and children, and was promptly stripped*

of my hejab. *Now being behind closed doors, the women could actually show themselves and be themselves. For women, there is a dimension of freedom by removing the* hejab. *So much of her body is covered in public, so much is forbidden and repressed, that when the scarf falls, there is a heightened sense of excitement.*

We had dinner, and attempted to have some girl talk. What I have found out to be the two big questions I have been faced with time and time again here from both men and women is, Am I married, and how many children do I have? At first I was truthful, but I had to withstand barrages of "Why not?" and "You are too old to be single!" Then I did the half truth: married but no children. This seemed to upset people even more, "But why no children? This is what women do! No children, no good!" Then I went with "I am married with four children," and I received kisses, handshakes, and cries of jubilation. What we may find chauvinistic and backward in the west is plainly embraced and accepted here.

For dinner I was hand-fed chicken by the mother of the bride. To be polite of course I allowed this to happen, but I dreaded what condition my stomach would be in tomorrow. If you didn't know, Arabs don't use toilet paper; they use their left hand to wipe themselves. We affectionately call your left hand your "dookie" hand. It is a terribly convenient way to contract E Coli as you can imagine.

After our meal the party really started. A heavy middle-aged woman named Farat *stood up and began to sing the most beautiful melodic Muslim songs. We sang along, clapping in unison, and took turns dancing in the center of the room. The dancing was very sensual,* Farat *thrust out her pendulous breasts, threw her head back, and put her arms over her head. She moved, swaying and undulating her way around the room. She outlined the curves of her body with her hands and beckoned us to join* her. *The women and children hooted and whistled as though we were male strippers, and even went so far as to throw Iraqi Dinars and candy at us. A few of the women started chanting in English "I am a disco dancer", which was my cue to show them the latest dance moves from 50's, 60's, and 70's. A few days later I picked up the ladies some dance club hits CDs from the PX which delighted them beyond belief. Western music is forbidden here, but is much sought after.*

After about three hours of dancing we heard AK-47 gunfire from outside. All the women scrambled for their hejabs *in a frenzy, indicating a man must be coming in. I was even helped to get dressed with a young girl, even tucking my hair under the scarf to make sure not even a strand was showing. For a brief moment I felt what it was like to be a Muslim woman.*

The groom entered the room and directly walked over to the bride, grabbed her by the hand, and led her into the adjacent room and closed the door. At this point, the singing, dancing, and clapping fell into a crescendo as the couple consummated their marriage not ten feet away. We sung fertility songs I later found out, and moved and clapped to the rhythm of the union of a husband and wife. I could figure out where this was going at this point, and yes, ten minutes later the groom emerged with a bloodstained sheet for everyone to see he married a virgin. There were cheers and applause, and almost a sense of relief that thus far their marriage was a success.

Now came the second round of celebratory gunfire. I was urged on to shoot by the chants of over a hundred Iraqi men. It is forbidden for a Muslim woman to shoot, but they were delighted at the spectacle of an American woman dressed in the hejab *shooting.*

I can only hope that the time I have spent with the local people throughout my deployment has some measure of influence

*over the Muslim attitude towards the United States, women,
and freedom.*

    Leyla

As we walked to our truck to leave, everyone in the village started chanting over and over in English, "GO, GO MISTAH!"

It was meant as a compliment, not in an attempt to tell us to leave their village or anything like that. We felt a little guilty, in that our very presence in their village was upstaging the wedding celebration a bit. We drove away slowly, smiling and waving, and thanking them for the invitation to share such a wonderful cultural celebration with them.

DAY 241: FRI 9 JAN 04

Captain Simmons finally left Najaf. The 900th Military Police (MP) Company relocated to Umm Qasr to run the detention facility there. An MP platoon from Karbala would be sent down every other day to track the Iraqi police until another MP Company from the States arrived at the end of the month to backfill the 900th.

We went to Camp Baker to meet with the new platoon leader and introduce ourselves. First Lieutenant Sattelmeier had blonde hair and blue eyes that went with his baby face. He was practically a twin of the 900th's own Lieutenant Odea. The Iraqi police would surely take to him. Perhaps they would even call him "the beautiful one" like they did Odea.

We went into the Tactical Operations Center (TOC) and sat around a table and briefed him and his NCO in Charge on the goings on in and around Najaf. This time, we seemed to get things off on the right foot. Hopefully it would remain that way for the duration of our deployment.

We went over to the school across from the Kufa mosque to see if we could get a good recording of Sadr's sermon for the week. Upon our arrival, we noticed that part of the wall around the school had been knocked down somehow, making the inner courtyard insecure. We drove past and turned around to head back. As we drove past, I noticed a couple of *Mahdi* Army soldiers standing on the roof of the school looking at us. It appeared that we would never use that school again. Since we had nowhere else to go that we could consider secure enough to record the sermon from, we headed home. There would be no sermon report for General Sanchez this week.

DAY 242: SAT 10 JAN 04

We drove to Camp Babylon to drop me off for my R&R leave. An hour later, I loaded up into one of the SUVs for the next leg of the trip to Baghdad International Airport (BIAP). Our interpreter named C+10 drove. We called him that because his name was so long and difficult to pronounce, we just called him C+10, denoting the number of letters in his name. Specialist Sebastian rode behind him. Captain Oliver rode shotgun, and I sat in the back seat behind him.

Some of my other team members had told me their own horror stories of their trips to BIAP with this bunch. They drove at reckless breakneck speeds, pointed their weapons at any vehicle that tried to pass them, and even chased dirt-clod throwing kids through fields that had not yet been cleared of mines. They had even fired shots into the hoods of vehicles that came too close to them on the highways, and fired into the air when children made threatening gestures at them. They drove so fast that other U.S. forces felt threatened, and pointed their weapons at them.

I was able to confirm at least one of those stories. Once we made it onto MSR (Main Supply Route) Tampa, AKA Highway 1 heading north to Baghdad, C+10 pegged out the speedometer at 200 kilometers per hour, the equivalent of 120 miles per hour—and kept it there. To prevent fratricide, they would place a DCU (Desert Camouflage Uniform) hat on the dashboard when approaching Coalition convoys, and then remove it again after passing them.

Two hundred Ks was definitely too fast. Since they were already going maximum speed, they had no acceleration left if they needed to get out of a kill zone. Their reaction time at that speed was nil. One sharp turn of the wheel to avoid something thrown into the road, and we would have flipped and rolled. At that speed, there would have been no survivors, even with seatbelts.

No one in Iraq wore seat belts because they didn't want to have to fiddle with the mechanism or worry about it getting hung up on their equipment if they needed to exit the vehicle quickly under fire. We routinely drove at high speeds ourselves on the highways, but only at about 120 kilometers per hour. This gave us some reaction time and reserved some power for acceleration if needed. It reminded me of the public service announcements on television back in the States put out by the National Highway Safety Board, trying to educate everyone that "speed kills." In Iraq, speed was more likely to *save* you, as long as it wasn't a reckless speed.

We arrived at BIAP and entered the sprawling base. We passed by the compound of Task Force 121 (TF121), the detachment from Delta Force that had killed Uday and Qusay, and had captured Saddam the previous month. We passed by another small detention facility where there was an Iraqi prisoner running around the prison yard with a sandbag on each shoulder under the supervision of some of the guards. I learned later that he was being punished because he refused to follow instructions. All of the Iraqi prisoners are told to keep their head and eyes down and not to look up at the guards, especially the female ones. But many of them were still too proud, and refused to listen to the female guards.

We pulled into the battalion headquarters, and I unloaded my bags. The headquarters was less than a hundred meters from the flight line, and there was a bunker nearby. I walked up the angled wall of the bunker to get a view of the flight line, and saw the C-5 Galaxy cargo plane that had been struck by a shoulder-fired missile shortly after take-off just a few days prior. The pilots had quickly turned the plane around and made a successful emergency landing. At the moment, there was a group of mechanics working on the number four engine where the missile had struck.

Later that day, I noticed several Humvees around BIAP that sported doors cut from steel plate. This cropped up as a local solution for the large number of unarmored Humvees in the country. Iraqi metalworkers were hired to cut doors from steel sheets for mounting on Humvees, to protect Soldiers from bomb blasts and gunfire. It was a winning solution for everyone, and another fine example of American ingenuity.

While I thought that I was leaving the following day, I discovered that I was actually not scheduled for three more days. The company had decided to bring me a few days early, as they were dropping off another Soldier that was going on R&R before me, and they didn't want to make another trip. On the other hand, my team back in Najaf was grounded and unable to collect or report intelligence because they didn't have enough people to operate. It was not a very resourceful operation. But at least we were getting to go home on leave, even at the expense of the mission, which was quite a sacrifice for the Army to make for us.

CHAPTER 7

ASHURA

SUN 1 FEB 04

My R&R leave had ended too soon. It wasn't enough time for me to catch up on everything that I had hoped to. But I did accomplish about 90 percent of everything that I had wanted to. One more week would have been perfect. Either way, I was glad to have had the opportunity, and it did wonders for my family and me. Sadly, though, my wife had shunned me: she feared that bonding with me would be counterproductive, knowing that I would be leaving again to return to Iraq. She felt that the pain would have been too much for her to bear.

After a few hours of waiting in the gate area of the airport, the plane arrived, and we boarded an old Lockheed 1011. It showed its age—there were still ashtrays on the bathroom doors. The venerable L-1011 wasn't flown by many commercial airline companies any more. There weren't any overhead storage bins down the middle of the plane for the center row passengers, so there was never enough room for carry-on luggage. We could hear the compressor blades on the number one engine rattling when they rubbed against the side of the engine cowling as the breeze passed through them. It sounded like a giant ball bearing rattling around inside the engine—which was a bit unsettling.

We took off on a clear afternoon, and I had a window seat where I could see the streets below. The bay was frozen over with a thin layer of ice in broken sheets that looked like a giant jigsaw puzzle. We headed out over the Atlantic as we reached our cruising altitude. The Atlantic was overcast below us, and the clouds were swirling in large circles, making them look like large frosted buns.

It would be a short night as we flew east against the rotation of the Earth. It quickly grew dark, and a few hours later we arrived over the lights of Paris, and descended into Frankfurt. Due to the time zone change, it was already 0500, almost dawn. We stayed in the terminal only about 45 minutes for refueling and a crew change, then continued on to Kuwait. I slept restlessly, and breakfast was served at noon.

Out the window, we were flying over the deserts of eastern Egypt, then we crossed the east coast and out over the Red Sea, and then over the shore and into western Saudi Arabia. From my vantage point at 35,000 feet, the desert looked beautiful. All of the various shades of brown and red, the wadis and black mountains, the roads and highways, small villages and desert towns. I could even see individual cars driving down the highways, seemingly out in the middle of nowhere.

Against the occasional clouds, the combination rainbow shadow of our aircraft stood out like the halo on a painting of the Virgin Mary. There were clouds like long ribbons lying parallel to each other, created by the varying temperatures at different altitudes. Down below, I could make out giant green circles of crops in the middle of the desert, irrigated by long pipes spewing water as they rotated around a single axis in the center.

Cities stood out like beacons against the bleak landscape, as almost all of the buildings were painted white to reflect as much of the sun's heat as possible during the hot summers. A single white contrail from another long-gone aircraft crossed below us like a never-ending ribbon from one horizon to the next, its dark shadow cast on the ground like a matching black ribbon below it.

As we approached the east coast of the Saudi peninsula, we turned north and followed the Persian Gulf shoreline towards Kuwait. Below were dozens of oil pumping stations and storage tank farms. We began descending, and circled over Kuwait City to make our approach, passing over the smoke stacks of the power station next to Camp Doha.

After circling over the Gulf, downtown Kuwait City came into view, with its high rise hotels and office buildings, and needle-like radio tower. As we crossed the coastline again, I could make out the wide streets that circled the city in huge rings. As we came in for our landing, passing over houses and apartment complexes, every rooftop was covered with satellite dishes, except for the large white mosque, which was capped with a large dome and cradled a pair of matching minarets on each side.

We touched down and taxied to the military end of the airport, passing by a ramp with a number of U.S. Air Force cargo planes. We parked and unloaded onto the flight ramp. There was another airliner in front of us in the process of unloading its planeload of Polish soldiers and their personal equipment.

In my absence, Camp Wolverine had added several truck-loads of gravel to strategic spots, and some landscaping had been done to divert the flow of water from rainstorms away from the tents. The chow hall had honey Dijon salad dressing—the only such salad dressing I had seen in the Middle East—as well as a sandwich bar, a make-your-own pizza bar, a dessert bar, an ice cream bar, and fresh popcorn available in grab-and-go bags. As I sat and ate dinner, a number of civilians were hooking up rows of televisions to satellite dishes in preparation to show the Super Bowl, which would be airing live early the next morning. Outside, a large outdoor projection screen was also being erected. On the tables were flyers announcing the arrival and visit of the famous pro athlete Bo Jackson, who was due to visit within the hour.

DAY 246: MON 2 FEB 04

In an effort to get my body clock readjusted to the eight-hour difference in time zones, I decided to stay up and watch the Super Bowl live. The game started about two A.M., and ended during breakfast. As I exited the Morale, Welfare and Recreation tent, the sun was rising.

Our C-130 ride to Baghdad International Airport (BIAP) was due early afternoon. As I waited in our tent with the rest of the Soldiers in my chalk, a group of them discussed WMD. One Soldier mentioned that five drums of mustard agent had been located on his camp. Another said that VX and Sarin nerve agents had been found on his camp. I didn't know which camps they were from, but from the sound of it, it seemed that there was more to the WMD situation in Iraq than was being reported by the press.

Our plane arrived, and we bused out to the ramp and loaded aboard. After we were buckled in, one of the load masters informed us, "There have been reports of possible air threats from missiles today, so we will be using evasive maneuvers into BIAP." I was not concerned. Not a single fixed-wing aircraft had been successfully shot down in Iraq. Unfortunately, helicopters had been another story. After staying up all night, I felt pretty tired, and tried to doze off during the short flight.

I awoke to the jolt of the tires hitting the runway. It had been an oddly smooth flight. Even though I was dozing, I had been anticipating the evasive maneuvering that the crew had told us to expect on our approach into BIAP, but it never came. I looked at my watch; we were ten minutes early.

I thought perhaps the flight was a bit shorter because we had taken a straight-in approach instead of evasive maneuvering. As I looked around the cargo bay, I saw a black female Soldier in the back of the bay lying on the floor. Her feet were elevated and her boots unlaced. Apparently, she had had some sort of medical condition during the flight. As we taxied to the parking apron, the load master lowered the rear ramp of the aircraft. As I looked out, the features looked strangely familiar—we were back in Kuwait. When the Soldier had passed out, the crew had turned the plane around and returned instead of continuing on to Baghdad.

An ambulance met the plane at the parking ramp, and the female Soldier was taken to the clinic. The rest of us were instructed to unload the plane and return to our tent to await further instructions, as the plane was now being given another mission. Once we had all shuffled back to the tent, we were then told that we would not be flying out until the next morning.

At 2000, we were told to grab our bags—suddenly there was a plane for us this evening after all. Once again, we bused out to the parking ramp and loaded into another C-130. Then the loadmaster, a master sergeant, announced to us, "There will be absolutely no electronic devices operated during this flight because they interfere with the aircraft's defensive systems, and that would be a bad thing. Once we are airborne, do not get up and walk around, as we will be flying in blackout conditions. The interior of the plane will be completely blacked out for light discipline." This sensibly followed the old adage that if the enemy couldn't see you, then they couldn't hit you.

As we approached BIAP, the plane made a few erratic maneuvers and spirals, but the landing was pretty smooth. It was about 2200 when we arrived. Since our flight had been rescheduled, no one was expecting us, so there were no buses to take us anywhere. I tried to call the battalion, but all of the phone lines were busy. I decided against waiting in the terminal until something happened, and opted for a proactive approach. I grabbed my duffle and backpack, and started walking to the gate. It was only about a mile to the battalion. The roads were muddy, but if I was lucky, perhaps someone would stop and offer a ride.

Before I even made it to the gate, a Humvee drove up from behind, coming from the direction of the terminal, and stopped. A couple of sergeants from the 1-1 Armored Cavalry offered me a lift, and dropped me right in front of the battalion. They were the example of Soldiers taking care of Soldiers, and I thanked them for their hospitality.

DAY 248: WED 4 FEB 04

As I awoke and went outside at dawn that morning, I saw a red AK tracer arc across the sky to the north. A few moments later, a loud *KARUMP…KARUMPKARUMP* echoed from across the south side of the base. It sounded like 120mm mortar rounds impacting. I ran up to the top of the bunker to see if I could make out any smoke, but in the thin morning fog, I couldn't see anything.

Out on the edge of the flight line about a hundred meters from me, an air raid siren blared from loudspeakers, followed by an immensely loud broadcast of "CODE RED, CODE RED, TAKE COVER, TAKE COVER!" I found it a bit comical that our own Air Force felt that the sounds from the explosions from impacting artillery rounds weren't sufficient warning for their personnel to take appropriate measures, and that they felt that they had to be instructed by loudspeakers before knowing what to do. No such warning system was in place for the Army. Despite the loudspeaker warning, no one was up and running for any of the bunkers. The sprawling base continued in its early morning slumber.

I went to the restroom, and saw a couple Soldiers calmly shaving at the sinks. "No one runs to the bunkers any more when there's incoming?" I asked.

"Naw, that only applies to the Air Force," one of them

replied. They continued to slowly drag their razors across their faces without even a hint of concern.

About ten minutes later, the loudspeakers came on again, "ALL CLEAR, ALL CLEAR." But how did they *know* that there were no more incoming rounds? What if the enemy was waiting to hear the all clear as a signal to fire a few more rounds? The loudspeaker certainly was loud enough. I had to smile and shake my head.

That afternoon, I was picked up by Captain Diebold, a transportation officer that was responsible for coordinating logistics for the Multi-National Division. Since all of the Coalition forces were fully supported by the United States, an American officer had to make all of the coordination for flights and cargo. Captain Diebold was one of those coordinators. He had come up from Camp Babylon to drop off an officer named Colonel Tiso. The colonel, with his 31 years in service and joking that he was the most senior-ranking colonel in all of Iraq (which he probably was), was being transferred back to CENTCOM headquarters at McDill AFB, Florida, and had to be dropped off at the Republican Palace complex in the Green Zone to catch his flight home in the next few days.

In the front seats of the SUV with Captain Diebold were a couple of Bulgarian Army officers who had been kind enough to drive him over from the far side of the sprawling base to pick me up. We drove back over to the other side of the airfield and met up with Colonel Tiso, transferred into another SUV, and then headed for the Green Zone.

We locked and loaded as we left the base, but only drove a few miles before coming to the next set of barriers, marking the outer rim of the Green Zone. The Hesco barriers went on for about a mile, and the road was lined on both sides with multiple strands of concertina wire. We passed by several high rise apartment complexes that looked down on the road we were traveling, and then passed by a large palace-like structure that used to be the *Ba'ath* Party National Headquarters. Beyond that, the airfield was surrounded by high concrete barriers, blocking all views of it from the road. On the right side was the Republican Palace, Saddam's primary residence and place of official business during his 24-year reign. It currently contained the offices of Ambassador Bremer and General Sanchez and their respective staffs, and was one of the sites being considered for the new U.S. Embassy. We parked in the lot on the left. Colonel Tiso went into the palace to find a room, while a couple of the officers carried his bags. The colonel carried his folding-stock Swiss-made 5.56mm SiG sub-machine gun (SMG) that he told me had been issued to him by CENTCOM for personal security detail duties.

It was a beautiful, bright, warm afternoon. MEDEVAC helicopters flew past overhead, landing at the hospital beyond the lot, and a pair of MH-6 helicopters with snipers in the doorway flew in circles over the palace complex. I watched through the trees across the street as dozens of people came and went from the palace, mostly Americans in civilian clothes, many women. It was like being back in the States. CIA and Delta teams came and went, evident by the multi-antennaed SUVs filled with mature-looking fit men with facial hair and civilian clothes, and toting exotic sub-machine guns.

Almost an hour later, the officers returned with stories of how unbelievable it had been inside the palace grounds. The inside of the palace was immaculate. The gardens were perfectly landscaped, and there was a large swimming pool behind the palace. The colonel had a room in the Distinguished Visitors' (DV) billets overlooking the pool. Perhaps this was part of why so many people compared the Green Zone to an aquarium, and claimed that no one inside the Zone had a clue what was going on in the rest of the country. The entire complex was surreal, and if you lived there, it was easy to see how you were so cut off from everything else going on outside—just like Saddam was when he was there.

On the ride back to Camp Babylon, Captain Diebold

filled me in a bit on what had transpired during my absence. He was working on transportation for an entire Iraqi battalion from Baghdad to Najaf. The battalion of Iraqi soldiers would then surround the Kufa mosque, and force Sadr's hand to either capitulate or strike back with his *Mahdi* Army. Either way, he would be removed and out of the picture. I was elated—it seemed the generals were finally heeding the advice I had been broad-siding them with in our team's reports to get rid of him. In the previous months they had been too timid to do anything about him, fearing that any interference of Sadr by the Coalition would spark a civil war in the *Shi'a*-dominated provinces of southern Iraq. He told me that I had returned from leave just in time.

We made it back to Camp Babylon by nightfall. Captain Oliver briefed me up a little further on what was being planned, and also informed me that while I had been on leave, the battalion commander had also gone home on emergency leave. In his stead, Major Baker was acting battalion commander. His first order was for the Bandits to turn in all of their non-standard weapons. During an earlier visit to B Company, he had seen some of the Iraqi weapons we used and reported them to the battalion commander, Lieutenant Colonel Duncan, urging him to have them all confiscated and brought to the battalion headquarters in BIAP. Captain Oliver informed Duncan that the weapons were on loan to us from the Marines that had left them in our care, and that they would want them back when they returned. That wasn't good enough for Major Baker.

Major Baker unjustly feared that one of our Soldiers would be tempted to try to smuggle one of them home. His fear was unfounded though, since we were all using the weapons on a daily basis, they were no longer exotic to us as they would have been to him or the other headquarters Soldiers in the rear who almost never left the base. None of us had any desire to take them home, especially since the penalties for weapons smuggling were steep.

Over Captain Oliver's objections that the teams were using the weapons daily to protect themselves, Major Baker insisted that they be consolidated and locked away. All of the teams had to bring in their AKs, where they had been locked up in the company arms room.

I was furious. The major had just put my Soldiers in increased danger because of his stupid biases against guns. I now had a team of Soldiers who would have to defend themselves with pistols against an enemy armed with machine guns and rocket launchers. He apparently had no clue about how the seven Spanish agents had died trying to defend themselves with their pistols while being shot to pieces from long range with assault rifles and rocket-propelled grenades. It was another prime example of field-grade incompetence and leadership-by-email from an officer that did not have a clue what it was like for the Soldiers on the front lines.

DAY 249: THU 5 FEB 04

Captain Oliver drove me to Najaf this afternoon. I had to pack my bags to be loaded into the conex back at Camp Babylon the following day. When it came time to leave, the company was planning on flying on a C-130 out of BIAP down to Camp Doha, Kuwait. But we would not be allowed to carry all of the bags each of us had on a C-130—there simply was not going to be enough space.

The company made their own travel arrangements to marry up with the rest of the battalion in Kuwait—they were not going to rely on the battalion to get them there because of all of the past logistical failures and other nightmares we had experienced. Just one example: to help replace worn-out uniform items from heavy wear and tear during deployment, the military issues additional uniforms and other clothing items to Soldiers after they have been deployed for six months, known as a "plus-up." Even though we had all submitted our sizes in December to receive the plus-up that had actually been owed to us in September, they never arrived. Another: while we had finally been issued the new army ballistic vests as promised by the Pentagon back in December, we still did not have any medium-sized vest armor plate inserts for them—hence they were still practically useless, unless the enemy shot at us with nothing more powerful than 9-millimeter pistol ammunition. Even worse, the battalion *never* issued the vests to C Company even after receiving them in December. C Company didn't even find out about the new vests until they had already deployed back to Camp Doha in March.

Upon my arrival back at the safe house, I learned that the entire THT from Diwaniyah had moved in with us. They had been tasked to provide field support to our operations in preparation for the upcoming moves against Sadr. Additionally, we had been assigned a new linguist to replace the two that I had to fire. His name was Moussa, and he was a Lebanese Christian, which made for a refreshing change from the two previous fundamentalist *Shi'a* Muslims that we had. We wouldn't have to interrupt operations any more in the middle of the day to bring them back to the safe house so that they could get in their five prayers a day, so that—as they told us—they wouldn't miss out on their guaranteed 72 virgins when they reached heaven. Also, Ali had been permanently reassigned to us from the Diwaniyah team. I was now responsible for a total of ten soldiers and linguists.

Fuwad was the Diwaniyah team's linguist. He was in his fifties, but still quite thin and fit. He told me one evening about how he had been born and raised in Iraq, and was drafted into the Iraqi army in 1971 for a 24-month tour. This was before Saddam had come to power in 1979, so he did not serve in the military under Saddam.

He was assigned to a Field Engineer unit stationed in Baghdad at the time. In the Iraqi army, being in an engineer unit meant that your equipment consisted of only two tools: a shovel and a pick. It was nothing but hard labor. There were no bulldozers, backhoes or other heavy engineering equipment.

The next day after being discharged from the hospital after having his stitches removed from surgery for a burst appendix, he learned that his unit had been reassigned to Airfield H3, way out in the western desert near the Jordanian border. He was ordered to take a commercial bus, which dropped him off on the side of the highway in the middle of the night, where the bus driver pointed him the general direction of H3—20 kilometers away—and told him to start walking. Because he had just been discharged form the hospital, he could barely walk from the pain of his incision, but he had no choice. On top of it all, he had to carry his two duffel bags. After walking 12 kilometers, he came across an anti-aircraft unit in the middle of the desert at about dawn. They put him in a vehicle and drove him the rest of the way to his unit at H3. But because he had reported in one day later than his expected arrival date, he was immediately thrown into the brig for seven days, and assigned to cleaning feces out of trenches left by the other soldiers. His seven days in the brig actually turned out to be a blessing in that the light labor actually gave him the opportunity to recover further from his surgery.

Upon his release from the brig, he was issued his pick and shovel, and was ordered to dig a trench one meter deep by one meter wide, 15 meters in length—per day. Every soldier in the unit had the same quota. The work day was from six in the morning until four in the afternoon, every day. If you hit a large rock or boulder in your stretch, you had to break it apart with your pick and keep going—it did not change your quota, even if you had to dig through the night. And you would start again the next day on time with the rest of the unit on your next 15-meter stretch. Even though it was certainly punishing, the digging wasn't punishment: the trenches were for burying data transfer cables running from the control building to each of the parking revetments for the Soviet-built MiG-23 and MiG-27 fighters that were assigned to the H3 air base.

The temperatures would reach 150 degrees. It was so hot and dry, that the desert flies would attempt to fly into any orifice on their bodies to obtain life-giving moisture, including into their eyes, up their nose, and down their throat if they left their mouth open. Sometimes just for fun, one of them would pour a tiny amount of water on the ground, and then they would watch as hundreds of flies from seemingly nowhere would instantly appear to try to drink it up before it evaporated within seconds from the scorching heat.

Fuwad lived in a tent with four other soldiers in his unit. They all ate from a large communal plate every night in the middle of the tent. They were served large portions of rice, and each one of them received a large raw onion which they ate like apples. He said that it was the best he had ever eaten up to that point in his life, and he actually gained 15 kilos during his assignment there. He must have been as skinny as a rail before then.

Each soldier was given only five gallons of water per *week* for drinking and bathing. For Americans, five gallons just for drinking water wouldn't last two days under those conditions, but he and his compatriots made it stretch for all seven days, week after week. As one can imagine, very little bathing was done.

They shared their humble accommodations with the large yellow and black scorpions that thrived there, growing up to six inches long. It was common to find three or four under your pillow before going to sleep at night. In the mornings, you had to vigorously shake out your boots before putting them on, and there would invariably be at least one inside them. Every night, at least one soldier in the unit would get stung by a scorpion, and would have to be rushed to the clinic for anti-venom.

It was at this point that Fuwad learned about the donkey-sized wolves that prowled the desert in those regions at night.

One man from the unit tried to run away, and all they found were his bloody clothes the next morning, 20 kilometers from the base—he had been torn apart and devoured by a pair of wolves. It made him think about his first night crossing the desert alone at night just to reach this place.

As they dug their trenches, they kept coming across pieces of pottery and statues from some ancient city that had stood at one time on that same place thousands of years ago. They would line up the dozens of artifacts along the top of the trench where they were digging every day, and their lieutenant would collect them all up, and they would never be seen again. He probably sold them on the black market. In the end, Fuwad said that he had loved all of it. In the early eighties, he had emigrated to the United States, and later became a U.S. citizen.

At about noon, a *Mahdi* Army assassin that had earlier managed to work his way onto Ayatollah Sistani's bodyguard detail attempted to blow Sistani up with a grenade. The would-be assassin was caught at the door by Sistani's real bodyguards.

DAY 250: FRI 6 FEB 04
Sistani's office denied that any attempt had been made on his life the previous day. Sistani was trying to cover it up because he didn't want his followers to take independent action against Sadr because he still respected Sadr's family, and was trying to prevent further bloodshed. Sami speculated that one way the Coalition could solve our problems would be if Sadr killed Sistani, then the Coalition would remove Sadr, thereby eliminating both problems.

DAY 253: MON 9 FEB 04
We picked up one of our informants and drove to Karbala to plug a location with the GPS and get some photos of a possible safe house/hideout for Hassani, the same guy who was

responsible for killing the MPs in Karbala back in October. The Coalition was still looking for this guy, and still wanted to take him out. We had found an informant who claimed to know where he was hiding. We were going to meet up with our counterpart in Karbala when we arrived there.

When we reached the city, we discovered that a number of the roads had now been blocked off with new Hesco barriers, and traffic was now re-routed all over the place. We had to drive down several different roads and then backtrack a few times before we found the entrance to one of the Coalition bases. We drove up to the gate very slowly, so as not to incite any suspicion from the Iraqi and Bulgarian guards. The gate guards in all of the Karbala bases were very touchy after the car bombings in December, and would not hesitate to open up on any vehicles that they felt were approaching the gates in a suspicious manner.

After reaching the gate, we discovered that none of the Bulgarian soldiers spoke English or Arabic. The Iraqi terps assigned to the gate explained to us about how difficult it was even for them to convince the Bulgarian soldiers that it was OK for other Iraqis who legitimately worked on their camp so that they would be allowed to enter. Right now, it was impossible for us to explain to them that we required entrance to meet up with our team. Finally, after about ten minutes of wrangling, one of them escorted me into the camp to their TOC to find a Bulgarian officer that could translate for us.

We walked about a hundred meters around several Hesco barriers and entered a building with a Bulgarian army armored infantry fighting vehicle parked out front. Inside the courtyard of this building, dozens of Bulgarian soldiers were suiting up as if they were preparing for battle, donning their vests, helmets, checking their weapons, and conducting other pre-combat checks. We weaved through the crowd and found an officer who addressed me in English. I explained to him our dilemma, and he replied, "No problem, we will have a car escort you to where you need to go. It is on another camp not far from here."

By the time I reached the gate, a Russian-made UAZ-469 staff car was behind me pulling out, loaded with armed Bulgarian soldiers. We loaded back into our trucks and followed them as they weaved through town for several blocks, stopping traffic by waving their arms and beating on the side of their staff car with their hands as they went, and we arrived shortly thereafter at another of the camps. At the gate was Rob, waving at us as we drove in.

We married up with them inside the compound, and talked over our plan. The Karbala team had a nice local van with tinted windows that was ideal for driving through busy areas without being noticed. A few more Soldiers would follow for security in another vehicle with curtained windows. I rode in the back to provide rear security to our little group.

We headed into town, and as we approached the shrine area, the traffic became very thick, and the streets became very narrow, only a single lane wide. As we drove down one narrow alleyway, another car parked directly in front of us, and the driver got out and walked away, blocking us and all of the traffic behind us. As we liked to say when we saw something totally senseless, "it was the Iraqi way." Fuwad jumped out and tracked down the driver and told him to move his car immediately. Ten minutes later we were slowly moving again.

We passed by the front of one of the two golden-domed shrines, and headed down a few more streets before we found our target. We plugged a grid with one of our GPS receivers, and took a few discreet photos as we drove past. At one point, we thought that there was a car that was following us that may have been part of Hassani's security detail, until it passed by us without notice. It was from his security detail, but the occupants didn't show any indications that they noticed us. With our mission complete, we went back to the camp, thanked our Karbala comrades, and headed back to Najaf.

As far as we could tell, nothing actionable was done with the intelligence that we had gathered on this mission. We never did find out whether Hassani had actually been there or not. Hassani was eventually captured in Karbala by U.S. Forces on June 15th.

DAY 258: SAT 14 FEB 04 VALENTINE'S DAY

As we were visiting one of the police stations in Najaf, a bus containing four cop-killer suspects drove up to the station and dropped them off. They were suspected of killing one of the Imam Ali shrine police officers with two shots to the chest from a pistol at close range. The leader of the group was from the *Mahdi* Army, and the other three were shop merchants who had been ordered to relocate away from the shrine by the shrine police for security reasons. This had been their way of protesting.

DAY 260: MON 16 FEB 04 PRESIDENT'S DAY

Local elections were scheduled to be held in Najaf the following day. There was a meeting with the MPs, the Spaniards and Salvadorans, many of the police chiefs and other local officials about security at the Najaf police station. When the meeting adjourned, Lieutenant Colonel Hayes, the 716th MP Battalion commander emerged from the doorway. When he saw me, we shook hands, and then he looked around and told me, "Why don't you step over behind my Humvee with me for a second."

We walked around to the back of the vehicle away from the Iraqi police. "Have you heard anything about upcoming operations?"

"No, sir, I haven't, not since a couple weeks ago about bringing an Iraqi battalion to town to shut down the *Sharia* court by the Ali shrine."

"Well, the current plan is to bring in a contingent of Iraqi police from out of town tomorrow under the cover of providing extra security for the elections. If the mission is a go, then starting around 2300 tomorrow night, they will go into the shrine area and take control of the *Sharia* court. By dawn, the goal is to have a local police outpost on the premises. So, the people will go to bed, and then wake up the next morning, and there will be no more *Sharia* court. But keep this close, we are not even telling the local police." It only made sense, since we knew that they were all courting Sadr anyway.

DAY 261: TUE 17 FEB 04

At around 0400 this morning, a video store in town was bombed for allegedly selling pornography. This was a common occurrence in *Shi'a*-dominated areas: when certain militaristic elements observed something that they felt was inappropriate or inconsistent with what they believed was allowed by the Koran, they would destroy it. It happened to restaurants in Baghdad that reportedly sold liquor to customers as well.

While meeting with some police officers later that morning, one captain begged me with concerned eyes, "Please save our country."

"That's why we're here," I tried to reassure him.

"It's not enough. You won't be able to do it."

"We already got rid of Saddam. What more can we do?"

"Please, you must do everything that you can to save us."

"We are doing what we can, but we will need your help. We can't do it all ourselves. After all, this is your country, now more than ever."

"Yes, thank you," he smiled and shook my hand. He still wouldn't provide specifics of what he felt we needed to do. But it was apparent that he was concerned about his country, and was confused about whether we, the Coalition, could help or not. Only time would tell.

The Najaf city elections had been peaceful. There had not been any reports of violence at any of the 23 polling stations. On the other hand, turnout had been very poor. The people were not happy with the choices that were available to them to vote for. Only four parties had fielded candidates, and none of them seemed appealing to the populace. The people were pessimistic and apathetic about democracy.

Had we, the Coalition, done a poor job in preparing and training the Iraqi people for democracy? The elections in Iraq were contracted out to a corporation called RTI from the United States. They had a team of about a half dozen people working on elections in our province, not counting their security detail. I did not have sufficient contact with any of them to know myself about the specific challenges of implementing Iraqi democracy.

The operation to shut down the *Sharia* court was postponed for 24 hours. We'll see if anything happens tomorrow night.

DAY 262: WED 18 FEB 04

At about 0715, two trucks, loaded with a total of about 700 kilograms of C4 plastic explosives, charged the front gate of Camp Charlie, the Multi-National Division logistics base in Hilla. As the trucks attempted to enter the camp, soldiers opened fire, preventing them from going any further. The first truck exploded under the gunfire, and the second blew up after hitting a concrete barrier.

The bombs killed 11 Iraqi civilians, which were probably made up mostly of camp employees waiting at the gate to go to work, but some were Iraqi women and children as well. 102 people were wounded, 58 of which were Coalition soldiers, including 26 Poles, as well as Hungarians, Bulgarians, Filipinos, and one American. Only six of the 58 required hospitalization. The rest were wounded by flying debris and glass, and the wounds were not considered life-threatening. The blasts flattened 11 nearby homes, damaged several more, and shattered windows as far as three miles away.

It had been the third suicide bombing in eight days. The

previous two had killed over a hundred other people. Such bombings had killed over 300 people since the beginning of the year, mostly other Iraqis. It fit with their tactics: use the first car bomb to blow a hole through the gate defenses, then try to drive a second car bomb through that hole and into the camp, and detonate it there in an attempt to inflict maximum damage. Fortunately, it didn't work this time. But they were getting closer to Najaf. With only about three weeks to go before we were scheduled to leave for Kuwait, we all hoped that if—God forbid—it happened, it would be after we were gone.

The operation to take down Sadr's illegal *Sharia* Court had been delayed again, this time until early Saturday morning.

DAY 263: THU 19 FEB 04

ODA 532 packed up and left this morning on their long trip back to Fort Campbell, Kentucky. They were back filled by ODA 556. Each team only serves about four months, then rotates home for four months, then deploys again. ODA 532 already knows that they will be back to Iraq in July.

DAY 264: FRI 20 FEB 04

I had the opportunity to speak with a Marine at Camp Babylon that had been present at the car bombing two days prior. He described how there were body parts from the dead scattered everywhere. It was believed that a hand was found from one of the suicide bombers, and our Hilla team was going to go collect fingerprints from it for identification. First Sergeant Neill instructed them that because of rigor mortis, it may be necessary to actually cut the fingers off the hand to get the prints.

One Soldier I met described how it was actually more dangerous to wear the older flak vest that we had been issued when we first entered Iraq, because the 7.62mm round fired from the AK-47 has just enough power to pass through the front of the vest, but as it does so, the vest mushrooms the projectile, making it way more lethal to the Soldier. Then, as it passes through the Soldier, it impacts the inside of the back of the vest, but at this point has lost too much velocity to pass through again so it bounces back into the body, and inflicts even more damage. The vests actually end up killing the Soldier, where he would have been better off without the vest altogether, and letting AK rounds pass completely through the body as intact projectiles.

DAY 267: MON 23 FEB 04

The morning was clear with a light breeze, but teeth-chattering cold. It remained so until the afternoon, when the sun had finally warmed up the earth sufficiently to shake off the morning shivers. The city was bustling not only with the usual bus caravans of Iranian pilgrims, but several thousand were already arriving for the memorial of Hussein's martyrdom at the Battle of Karbala during the seventh century. Part of the events was supposed to include self-flagellation with chains, knives and even swords to the point of drawing blood.

As we drove through the city, large colorful flags were flying everywhere, and a number of tents for pilgrims had been set up along the sides of the roads. They were serviced by refreshment stands serving water and *chai*. Many were adorned with strings of lights, like many of us would do during the holiday season.

Anti-American graffiti decorated the inner perimeter wall of one of the police stations. It must have been fresh, as we had never seen it there before. And since it was on the inside, it had probably been written by one of the officers. Along the wall, someone had written "Down Amriky," a rough spelling of the Arab pronunciation of America, another said plainly "NO USA," and the next said "Down USA." Each was either smeared with mud or appeared that something had been used in a poor attempt to erase it from the wall, but they were still plainly visible. We would have to be a bit more vigilant at the police stations from now on. It wouldn't do any good for one of us to be killed, and especially by a police officer at this point in our deployment. We only had about two weeks left before we were supposed to move to Kuwait.

As we passed by the Traffic Police headquarters, about a hundred Iraqis were out in front, waving banners written in Arabic, punching their fists into the air and shouting furiously. We asked our interpreter Moussa if he could read what the banners said, and he told us that they were protesting that the traffic police chief was a former member of the *Ba'ath* party. It was true, but like so many others, he had renounced his membership. That didn't seem to matter to many people around here though. The Badr Corps had been hunting down and killing former *Ba'athists* for several months now, unrestricted by the Coalition. We had heard nothing about *Ba'athist* activity in our province for several weeks. They had either fled to Syria or been killed. The latest casualty was an Iraqi police officer who had been known to torture people during Saddam's regime.

We went to visit the MPs and report what we had seen, and I ran into Lieutenant Colonel Hayes, the MP battalion commander. He was showing around his replacement, Lieutenant Colonel Snyder, the incoming MP battalion commander from the Kentucky Army National Guard. They had also attended a meeting earlier that morning to determine what to do about Sadr's illegal court. The Coalition wanted the Iraqis to close it down with their own forces so that no one could say that the Coalition was against it. But the chiefs of police of Basra and Karbala both claimed that up to 40 percent of their police forces are pro-Sadr, and wouldn't conduct such an operation. The decision was made to postpone any further anti-Sadr operations for at least a month, and attempt to raise an independent police unit for just such a purpose, and then possibly disband it afterwards.

When I told the colonel about the demonstration, he asked, "Did you see any weapons?"

"No, sir, no weapons."

"Well, then let them demonstrate," he replied with a smile. He introduced me to Lieutenant Colonel Snyder, and I then went to go tell the MP platoon leader about the demonstration.

We were told that not only did Sadr run his own *Sharia* Court and secret underground jail that enforced Sadr's control over the local community under the guise of Muslim religious law, but now the Badr Organization also had their own court and jail. And supposedly there was even an agreement between them that the Badr Corps would transfer over any prisoners that had been apprehended on charges of working for, assisting or otherwise colluding with the Coalition to Sadr's underground court for "trial" and punishment. There was supposedly a jail in the basement of a building in old Najaf, and prisoners there were being tortured and executed.

We had reported on Sadr's illegal secret court and jail numerous times, but nothing was ever done about it, so it continued to operate and terrorize the local populace. The *Mahdi* Army had declared themselves the guardians of peace and justice, and established underground jails and courts outside the law in Najaf, Baghdad, and seven other southern cities. They went around shutting down liquor stores and stands, and even killing their owners. Najaf was already a dry province due to its religious significance, so there was no liquor publicly available here. Most people traveled to Diwaniyah for liquor. CD sellers accused of selling pornography—a broad category which included most western movies—had their shops bombed by the *Mahdi* Army. People caught drinking alcohol or having sex outside of marriage were strapped to a column and whipped. Even women and Iraqi Christians were not exempt from judgment and punishment by Sadr's courts. The underground cells were so small that it was impossible to stretch out. Air came in through a small pipe in the ceiling, and there was no light.

Supposedly, the only thing stopping Sadr from passing death sentences—as permitted by the *Koran*—was the presence of the Coalition. But this didn't always stop them. One woman was arrested for supposedly allowing prostitutes into her home; her body showed up ten days later with lash marks on her back and her fingernails torn out.

It was no secret that Sadr was using his so-called courts more to stamp out his enemies than to distribute true justice. But Sadr's shroud of religious legitimacy prevented the local police from taking any action. All of this went on despite General Sanchez's public statement that, "If there are any courts operating outside of the law, they're at risk of being shut down." Apparently, Sadr's risk assessment of General Sanchez's warning didn't faze him. With such sternly worded warnings, it was hard not to see why.

We drove past the Badr Corps headquarters building to get some photos and to plug a grid with our GPS. The building was a few miles from the Ali shrine, but still accessible to us. It was not inside any of the off-limits areas.

The traffic was so heavy from the upcoming *Ashura* holiday that cars, and even buses, were driving on the wide sidewalk running next to the wall around the world's largest cemetery. As we approached the building, the street in front was swarming with about 40 men armed with AK-47s. Most of them were just standing around, but a few of them were attempting to direct traffic. The building was large and surrounded by a steel grate fence. There were large red flags flying from the fence and gate, and a concrete pill-box bunker stood over the gate. There were men in the bunker, but no machine gun was visible. The building itself was adorned with a large poster of the martyr Hakim, the one killed by the Al Qaeda bomb blast just outside the Ali shrine last August.

We drove through the traffic and tried to turn around at

the next break in the median. Several *Badr* soldiers were there directing traffic, and the intersection was blocked by a number of buses. As we halted in the middle of the turn, several of the men saw us. An argument between a few of them broke out in the street directly in front of our vehicle. It appeared that they were arguing about how to direct the traffic to let us through, or possibly whether to kill us on the spot or not. Meanwhile, the other men were smiling at us, waving, and even saying hello. They did not react threatened by our presence, nor did any of them raise their weapons. They knew that they were in control, and that there was nothing we or anyone else in the Coalition was going to do to them. They knew that they had nothing to fear from us.

They were right. We would report what we had learned, and nothing would be done about it. They knew it as much as we did. Two more weeks, and then it would be someone else's problem. I could feel that I was beginning to get the short-timer's attitude, where you didn't care any more what did or did not happen, as long as it didn't interfere with your leaving and going home. We learned a few days later that the secret Badr jail had been a ruse, probably in an attempt to play off the Coalition against them.

A little further down the road, we stopped briefly at a rug shop and asked the merchant if he could bring his good stock out a few days later for us. They usually kept the good stuff at their homes, and you had to tell them in advance so that they would bring it to the store for you. We would then go back at an undetermined time later.

Our company headquarters showed up on an unannounced equipment inspection. We hadn't lost anything so it went rather quickly. Sami told them about the time he had dysentery several weeks ago and had defecated on himself while crawling to the bathroom. Sami thought it was a funny story.

Another report came in about five car bombs crossing

the Saudi border and coming to Najaf. Supposedly, Al Qaeda leader Abu Musab Al Zarqawi, Usama bin Laden's commander in Iraq, had met with either Sistani or Sadr, but no one knew which one or what had been discussed. Things were starting to look just a bit more dangerous here in quasi-peaceful Najaf. We could feel and see that the level of tension across the city was ratcheting up.

DAY 268: TUE 24 FEB 04

We went to the police station on Medina Street to visit one of the police officers there. Medina Street was the main artery of Najaf's business district, lined with shops of all kinds, and always teemed with traffic and people during the day. We drove on the side streets to get past some of the Hesco barriers, concertina wire and heavy traffic that surrounded the station. We received a number of stares as we drove the back roads. Very few Coalition vehicles drove around on the back alleys of the city.

As we turned onto one alleyway, we passed by a large black cloth billboard that someone had hung on the outer wall of their home. The people across the city were hanging up all sorts of colorful flags and posters for *Ashura*, the commemoration of the Imam Hussein's martyrdom at the battle of Karbala.

This particular billboard contained posters of Ayatollah Khomeini, Ayatollah Bakr Sadr, and a quite graphic resemblance of the Imam Hussein's head mounted on a pike over his headless corpse. And of course, there was the obligatory poster of Muqtada al-Sadr. Arabic writing on the black cloth over the posters translated as, "Even if our legs were amputated, we would still crawl to you, Imam Hussein."

We turned into the police station, which was dangerously situated right on Medina Street. While there were some Hesco barriers in front of the station, there were wide areas of open space on each side, blocked only by a curb and a single strand of concertina wire. There were two derelict Chevy sedans with flat tires sitting in front of the station as well, as if they were also barriers, but they were so far apart that they provided no extra protection. A suicide bomber could easily drive right into the station with little to stop him. Security here was weak.

The street in front of the station was teeming with people and traffic. A bit further down the street, several large colorful flags blew in the cold wind, hanging outside a mosque. There were puddles of standing water here and there, and garbage was strewn everywhere. Electrical wires cris-crossed overhead in all directions.

Some men climbed up on the roof of the building directly across from the station and tied a pole with a large red flag on it, decorating their store. Almost every shop on the street flew some sort of flag. A number of dirty children played around us as Paul, Moussa and I provided security while Joe had his meeting inside.

A lone white pickup truck pulled into the station. There were three Salvadoran soldiers riding in the bed of the truck with their M-16s pointing out. Another sat in the back seat with his barrel out the window. At the wheel was a Spanish army soldier. He drove into the station courtyard, but parked directly in the gateway as a security measure, so no other cars could get in or out. He was one of the Spanish intelligence officers, and had probably come to meet with one of his own informants. The Salvadoran soldiers were assigned to be his Personal Security Detail (PSD). Within a few minutes, they loaded back up and left. The Spaniard never spoke a word to any of us.

With the exception of the children, almost no one said hello to us as we stood outside the station. Even the other officers pretty much ignored us, which was unusual. The tension was thick. It was easy to tell that we were not really welcome there. Moods in the city were visibly changing.

The minaret from the mosque down the street started blaring noon time prayers over its loudspeakers. Shortly thereafter, Joe and Ali emerged from their meeting and we left.

Defense Secretary Rumsfeld had arrived in Baghdad the previous day, and publicly announced what we in the intelligence community had known for some time: Al Qaeda and other terrorist groups were infiltrating Iraq from their sanctuaries in Iran and Syria, and killing American Soldiers, although recently they were now focusing on other Iraqis.

DAY 270: THU 26 FEB 04

Ashura celebrations began this evening. I noticed something was different when the city was not filled with the sounds of gunfire and the blaring horns of wedding processions once the sun had gone down. Instead, almost every home was lit up with a string of white lights. In some places, entire streets were lit up like *Mardi Gras*, with strings of lights across the road down its entire length. Mats were set out and fires were lit. Families sat around together outside, some were heating water and sipping *chai*. The relative peace and tranquility of the city on what otherwise would have been a loud and bustling evening was odd, but welcomed.

DAY 272: SAT 28 FEB 04

Brigadier General Aziz, the Najaf chief of police, was incurring the wrath of his own officers across the city with his blatant corruption. The Coalition had issued the city a supply of *Glock* pistols, but instead of issuing them out to his officers, he was *selling* them to the officers for about 30 dollars apiece, which he pocketed. Those that didn't pay him didn't get their pistols.

What was worse was that officers that complained to us about it had their salaries cut. This interfered directly with our work, the safety of the city and the Coalition. We gathered up copies of all of their reports, added a cover letter requesting that the general be arrested, or at least removed, and gave it to Rick Olsen of the Coalition Provisional Authority, the only person with the authority to do so.

DAY 273: SUN 29 FEB 04 LEAP DAY

The Military Police conducted a raid on the "Little Chechnya" open weapons market this morning. There had been reports of weapons being sold on the open market. The raid had been jointly coordinated with and planned by the Iraqi Police, which meant that it was tipped off by officers loyal to Sadr. When we were expecting MP-5 submachine guns, the only things captured were a single AK and one PKC machine gun. No arrests were made. All the lucrative arms dealers had stayed home this morning.

There was a whole fleet of new trucks for the police at one of their stations. They were white Japanese-made king-cab pickups, just like the ones we had. Within ten minutes, some officers had come over to tell me that General Aziz had already been selling some of them on the street and pocketing the cash.

CHAPTER 8
LIBERATION

DAY 274: MON 1 MAR 04

The order finally came this morning. We are to report tomorrow at 1000 hours to meet the new THT that will be replacing us. For our last day of independent operations before our relief arrived, we did… nothing. It was to be our last day off as well. Everyone on the team packed footlockers and boxes to mail home one last time with all of the things that they didn't want to carry with them back to the States. Leyla and Sami packed the beautiful Persian rugs that they had bought down at the *Suuk*, the Arab market.

We were instructed to front-load all of the training for the new THT into the first four days, so that there would not be any reason for delay if we were ordered to depart earlier.

DAY 275: TUE 2 MAR 04 *ASHURA*

We drove to Camp Babylon and waited for the "replacement killers" to arrive. As we waited for their departure from Baghdad, we heard on the news about the suicide bombings around the shrines of Karbala, and one of the shrines in Baghdad, where thousands of pilgrims were honoring *Ashura*. Television coverage showed some of the actual explosions that had been caught on home video.

Ashura was the most sacred day of the year on the *Shi'ite* calendar. Over two million pilgrims from such countries as Iran, Pakistan, India, Lebanon, Uzbekistan and several other Gulf states had converged on Karbala over the past week to pray at the Imam Hussein's gold-domed tomb on this day. Under Saddam's rule, the celebration of *Ashura* had been banned, forcing pilgrims to perform their rituals in secret.

 Draped in the traditional white funeral shrouds signifying their readiness to accept their own martyrdom, men were the main celebrants of *Ashura*. Hussein's death is honored with re-enactments and ritual cutting of the scalp with knives or swords until the blood runs down their chests. Young men and even boys ritually flog themselves with whips or chains until their backs are bruised and bleeding. Others beat their chests to a cadence set by drums and cymbals, in a practice called *lutm*. Even though Imam Hussein was killed over 1,300 years ago, for the millions of *Shi'ites* celebrating *Ashura*, it could have happened only yesterday.

White Mercedes ambulances with orange stripes ferried exhausted pilgrims from the rituals in a rotating convoy between the shrines and the hospitals. Religious flags of green, red and black fluttered from houses along the way. Chants of mourning from minarets filled the air. Black banners featuring silver hands whose five fingers represent Hussein and his closest relatives were displayed from almost every building, along with posters depicting the gruesome beheading of Hussein and his abandoned warhorse, *Duldul*, always shown as a beautiful white yet battle-scarred stallion with his head hung low as if in mourning for his dead master. The day *Duldul* had wandered back and returned from the battlefield was the signal to his followers and family that the Imam Hussein had been killed.

Security in Karbala was being handled by religious volunteers and *Mahdi* Army members instead of Iraqi police. Traffic was stopped at several points outside the city, where these volunteers checked vehicles for explosives. Inside the city, they frisked pilgrims and rummaged through their bags. But the crowds were vast, and the searches became rushed in a hopeless effort to keep up with the ever-growing throngs. Pilgrims sat in silence before the shrines that morning reading prayers. Along the roads, huge steel vats of *harisa*, a stew specially made and served on religious holidays, were cooked over wood fires and blowtorches. Tea and water were also served free to pilgrims.

Starting at about ten that morning, the blood ritual gave way to the blood of atrocity. Six blasts rocked the city, each about a minute apart. One explosion that had been caught on a home video camera unleashed a hug fireball that whooshed down the street known as the Baghdad gate, the main entrance to the shrine area, which was overflowing with worshippers. It was quickly followed by a second blast from the far end of the street, propelling slivers of shrapnel and ball bearings into the crowds.

Victims dropped like stick figures as pandemonium reigned. No one knew where to run as the blasts kept coming. Women tripped over their long black *abayas* as they ran. The blasts came from at least one suicide bomber, who struck outside an elementary school, killing several Iranian pilgrims, including a mother and her young daughter, but also from TNT covered with nails and ball bearings that had been hidden along the narrow roads that were being used by the hundreds of thousands of worshippers.

People ran for their lives. Outside the Imam Musa al-Khadam shrine, the crowd dragged away a man after grenades had been thrown from a hotel window into the crowds. They beat him senseless as they went, shouting that he was a Yemeni.

At one city entrance, a tall, bearded man wearing a cape ran toward a crowd of pilgrims that were beating their chests in a ritual of mourning. He filtered into the middle of the crowd, yelled out *"Allahu Akbar!"* and detonated a belt of explosives.

The deafening blast threw his own head about 25 meters, his clothes flew upward, and scattered his own severed legs next to the bodies of his victims. Bodies, feet, arms and pieces of flesh were everywhere.

Their holy places had been profaned. But the bombings didn't stop the celebrations. Within four hours of the explosions, pilgrims once again began filtering down the roads to the shrines, passing by at least three of the blast sites, each marked by a mound of shoes and slippers from the dead and wounded.

At least 143 people were killed, including fifteen children, and over 400 injured. At least 22 of the dead were Iranian pilgrims. The final death toll was very likely significantly higher, as many of the bodies had been blown to small bits, and many others were taken directly for burial without being counted.

The attacks were at some of the holiest shrines in *Shi'ite* Islam and on the most sacred day in the *Shi'ite* calendar. Police in Basra had arrested four would-be suicide bombers—two of them were women wearing explosive belts.

In Najaf, our own Iraqi police had discovered and defused a car bomb the previous night. They had arrested a former Iraqi intelligence officer and two of his associates. The police interrogated him for 24 hours before he admitted working for Al Qaeda, and also gave up the names of four of his other associates. At the time of his arrest, he had been dressed as a police officer. He was later handed over to American forces. No one had even informed us of it.

The crowds in Karbala wanted to blame everyone except the people most likely to have been responsible for the attacks. One man even ridiculously claimed to have seen an Israeli jet fly over. No one seemed willing to draw the obvious conclusion that the bombers were fellow Arabs and Muslims. Zarqawi was carrying out his terrorist campaign as described in a letter he wrote. It had been found on a CD-ROM seized in a Baghdad raid in January 2004, outlining his plans to attack *Shi'ite* religious sites. The attacks were designed to provoke *Shi'ites* into fighting American troops and spark a sectarian war between the *Shi'ites* and the *Sunnis*. Zarqawi was open in his hatred of *Shi'ites*, describing them as the evil of mankind, and told his followers that they were the enemy.

Grand Ayatollah Sistani accused the Coalition of failing to provide adequate security for the worshippers and of not doing enough to prevent terrorists from crossing Iraq's porous borders. Administrator Bremer countered by stating that there were already 8,000 Iraqi border police on duty and that more were on the way, 60 million dollars had been committed to support border security, and we were adding hundreds of vehicles.

At first, the Iraqi Police claimed that it was a mortar attack, because were they to admit that it was suicide bombers, then that would have meant that they were not doing their jobs correctly. But the buildings around the bombings would not have allowed the trajectory of mortar fire. Some of the bombers were captured, still wearing their suicide vests.

The new Soldiers finally arrived after a three-hour delay in Baghdad due to the bombings. Their leaders had been afraid to take to the highways, not knowing what more to expect in the way of attacks. While we were expecting one team, we discovered on the spot that a second team had also been assigned to Najaf due to the city's importance to General Sanchez. There were eight counterintelligence agents assigned to Najaf now. Fortunately, we had the space in our safe house complex for them, but we had to take another vehicle from headquarters to fit all 15 of us and get back to Najaf.

We went to dinner in Najaf at Camp Baker, then walked through our safe house complex identifying all of the team equipment, and then planned the next day's activities. It had already been a long day. At least the transition had now begun. We were one step closer to going home.

DAY 277: THU 4 MAR 04

We took the new team on a tour of the city this afternoon. I wanted to show them the Imam Ali shrine. We had to pass through a traffic checkpoint at Revolutionary circle that was guarded by militia armed with AKs from the Badr Organization. At first, they wouldn't let us through, but as I persisted, and they eventually saw that I was U.S. military, they finally relented and let us pass.

It didn't matter much, though. As we approached the marketplace before the shrine, the street was blocked off again to all vehicle traffic. There was a serious threat from car bombs, and this was their method of dealing with it. Just beyond the road block, the street was filled with hundreds of pilgrims, roaming through the *suuk*. We turned around and went towards Kufa.

As we reached the Kufa police station, the main road was blocked off here by a large band of *Mahdi* Army thugs, all armed with AKs. They were physically stopping vehicles, and pulling people out and searching them and their vehicles. They acted a bit surprised to see us, but once they realized that we wanted through, they created a break in the line and let us drive through. We just smiled and waved, trying to appear non-threatening to them.

On the roof of the mosque directly across from the police station, the *Mahdi* Army had mounted an RPK machine gun—aimed at the police station. It was an ominous sign of things shortly to come. There was a large number of police officers milling around their own front gate, naturally doing nothing about the blatantly illegal activities being carried out by the *Mahdi* Army right in front of them. Every ten feet along the road was another *Mahdi* Army member with an AK, all the way down the road to the Kufa mosque. Families of Iranian pilgrims picnicked among the thugs just off the side of the road. In front of the mosque, there must have been about a hundred or so of them, all armed with assault rifles and sub-machine guns. One of our Soldiers saw one man with what appeared to be an RPG launcher rolled up in a rug.

Traffic was too heavy to turn back around and pass back through the area again, so we circled all the way back around past the cement factory to the other end of town. Later, we learned that Sadr had passed through a Salvadoran traffic checkpoint on the Kufa bridge at about midnight. He was in a convoy of seven cars, and had 15 armed bodyguards with him, all with American-issued weapons carry permits—obviously forged. Naturally, they let him continue on his way. Another prime opportunity to take Sadr into Coalition custody—probably the last one before the first battle of Najaf started in early April—slipped through our fingers.

DAY 278: FRI 5 MAR 04

We received a report that a taxi driver had brought in six Afghans that had been talking in his taxi about attacking the Coalition. He had driven them straight to the police station and turned them in. We went to talk to them this morning.

As we crossed the main road through the city, the intersection was guarded by three *Mahdi* Army thugs, one carrying an AK. This was the first time was had seen armed *Mahdi* Army west of Camp Baker. This was as far from Kufa as they had ever been. They were expanding their control over the entire city. As usual, nothing was being done about it by Coalition forces.

We entered the station and asked that the eldest of the six prisoners be brought to us for questioning. After we had talked to him for a while, we realized that he was either pretending to be nuts, or he really was nuts. He described how he loved Americans, and then in the same breath stated that he wanted to kill Bush. Then he explained how everything he owned came from the 50 angels that were around him at this very moment, to include the clothes he was wearing, to the million Saudi *Rials* he claimed he was going to pay the taxi driver to take him to Mehran, Iran. When we asked him how many people were in the taxi with him, he replied that it was only him. We realized that we weren't going to get anywhere with him, so we had him taken out and asked for another prisoner from the group.

The second prisoner explained to us how his uncle, the man we had just talked to, was indeed mentally ill, and that he and his brothers and nephew were all sitting quietly at home when the police barged in and arrested them all, and he had no idea why. We asked for a third prisoner, and specifically requested the youngest one in the bunch, who was a 15-year-old boy. He corroborated his uncle's story, and explained that his father really was a bit crazy.

We explained what we had discovered to the police officer in charge, and requested that he inform the judge at their hearing the following day. There was no threat against the Coalition here. Hopefully, they would all be released and back home by the end of tomorrow.

As we went to Camp Baker for lunch, we passed by the same *Mahdi* Army members on the corner, and then noticed that there were additional thugs posted every hundred feet or so down the main street, all the way to Camp Baker. Now it appeared that they had taken over the entire city. We reported it to the MPs in the chow hall, who seemed ambivalent about it. They were short to go home as well, and it wasn't really their mission to take armed thugs off the street. That was supposed to be the Spanish. But they could not be counted on to do much of anything at this point. At the intelligence meeting the previous evening, the MPs went off about how the streets were teeming with armed *Mahdi* Army, and insisted that the Spanish do their job and get them off the street. The only thing that the Spanish officer said was to request any further information about who had told the *Mahdi* Army that they could be on the street, as if that was somehow relevant.

As we left Camp baker, we saw three *Mahdi* Army members standing in front of the hospital. One was armed with an

AK. As we pulled up and stopped next to them, the second one handed a revolver to the third, who tried to walk away. We called him back over, and asked them who they were. They replied that they were *Mahdi* Army, and that they were doing their part to help protect the city. We told them that was the responsibility of the police, not them, and that they were not allowed to be on the street with weapons.

A bit further down, we came to a police checkpoint, and stopped to ask the ranking officer why he was allowing *Mahdi* Army on his street with weapons. He explained that they had been given strict orders some time ago from the police chief to leave the *Mahdi* Army alone.

We circled back around to inform the MPs again that armed *Mahdi* Army were now only a hundred meters from the Camp entrance. As we passed by, they were already gone. As we entered the camp, we saw another member across the street next to a large wooden box lying on the ground.

The MPs were already out visiting a number of police stations in the city. We decided to investigate the thug and his box ourselves, but when we went back out, he and his box were already gone, as were the rest of the ones along the entire street. The police checkpoint was also gone.

DAY 279: SAT 6 MAR 04

I was ordered that when we left, I was supposed to bring with me all of the Iraqi weaponry that we had been using, and the M-60 machine gun, which I had already signed over to the new team. They wanted it for convoy security from Hilla to Baghdad, when they admitted that they already had at least three other crew-served weapons for the trip. Even when I pointed this out to them, it didn't change their minds, and they continued to insist that I bring the weapons with me, and screw the team that was replacing us.

As soon as their trucks were out the gate and on their way to Karbala, I told the incoming team leader what had transpired, so that she could contact her leadership and let them know what was going on. This was an insensitive way to run a war.

General Sanchez had visited Camp Babylon a few days ago and met with all of the brigade commanders. He ordered them that Operation Law and Order would be implemented and completed within the next 30 days, which was the current plan to arrest Sadr and eliminate the *Mahdi* Army. When the Spanish brigade commander tried to raise his objections, the general shot him down on the spot, cutting him off mid-sentence and reiterated that it would be done. Sanchez's point fell on deaf ears.

This is what we had been pushing for since we started working in Najaf. Now it was looking like we would miss out on partaking of the results. That was fine with us—at this point, we were so fed up with the lack of action to the 300-plus intelligence reports that we had written and submitted about Sadr that we would rather go home anyway.

The chief of police, Brigadier Aziz, was fired today by the CPA—finally. At least now we would have some credibility with some of the citizens and other police officers in the city. It appeared that our recommendations were finally receiving some of the attention that they deserved.

DAY 281: MON 8 MAR 04

I took one of the new teams out to the ammo dump as part of their area familiarization, as well as to introduce them to the only other Americans in the province. Shortly after our arrival, they invited us out to the demolition range, where they were in the process of assembling one of the largest demolition shots to date.

They had gathered up about 200 tons of ordnance for destruction that day, consisting of a large collection of Russian-made helicopter-deliverable anti-personnel bomblets—the type that Saddam favored for dropping from his helicopters onto insurgents like the *Shi'ites* during the 1991 *Intifada*. General Schwarzkopf had made the self-admitted mistake of permitting Saddam to fly helicopters after the cease-fire signing, and Saddam had taken advantage of that loophole to bomb, strafe and attack rebels throughout Iraq. To that end, he used these bomblets to crush the rebellion.

These 159 canisters of bomblets were covered with Russian RDX plastic explosives. Next to these was a 50-foot long double row of artillery rounds stacked five high, each covered with a row of C-4 plastic explosive. A little further was the mother lode: a 40-by-40 foot square stack of mortar shells, artillery and tank rounds, and rockets, all stacked over two feet deep. The entire square was laced with rows of C-4 and det cord.

We drove out a little over three kilometers into the open desert from the range and waited for the ignition. There was a large and brilliant orange flash shot over a hundred feet high into the air. A giant gray and white cloud emerged from the flame, and red tracers flew up over the cloud like fireworks. A few seconds later, we were struck with a deafening "BANG!"

The cloud continued to rise over a thousand feet into the air, and we watched as it was blown away to the north by the winds at that altitude, and slowly dissipated.

The chief of the Customs police had invited us to a farewell dinner that evening, and we went to their favorite restaurant along Route 9 across from the cemetery. We all had a grand time. During the dinner, the restaurant owner's son tried to take some photos of us with his own digital camera from across the room. I mentioned it to one of the police officers, and they retrieved the camera from him, and we erased the photos that he had taken of us. We thanked each other for everything, and said our good-byes.

DAY 283: WED 10 MAR 04
The big day that we all had been waiting for had finally

arrived. We spent the morning packing our bags, while the new team was out in town meeting informants. Once they returned, we loaded our gear into the trucks. We drove over to the chow hall for one last lunch, then drove through town past the Kufa mosque one last time.

Ashura was over now, so the streets seemed deserted in comparison. There were no *Mahdi* Army on the streets any more, and traffic was very light. We drove through the market, crossed the bridge, and headed to Hilla.

Team leaders gathered for an After-Action Review, and to brief the officers of the new unit. Everyone briefed the same deficiencies for each team: lack of reliable communications, inability to get anyone to act on actionable intelligence and actually make arrests and conduct raids on weapons caches, lack of communication with the Multi-National Division, lack of logistical support from our own chain of command, among others. Despite these challenges, the Soldiers overcame them and still were able to accomplish their missions—not because of our chain of command, but in spite of it.

DAY 284: THU 11 MAR 04

Everyone reloaded the vehicles, and we had one mass convoy with 11 different trucks, vans and SUVs, fully packed with all of our gear. This was to be our last convoy though the Iraqi combat zone before leaving the theater, and we didn't want anyone to get hurt at this point. Extra M-16s were issued to those Soldiers who had only pistols. Two captured Russianmade RPK machine guns provided our crew-served weapon support requirement. As we were about to leave, we learned that the mail truck from BIAP had been turned back because of bombs along the highway.

We convoyed out and headed north on MSR Tampa towards Baghdad. The six-lane freeway made the trip very relaxing, but we still had to stay alert for anything unusual. One of the tactics that we developed to avoid being hit by debris or explosives dropped from overpasses was to jink left or right while passing underneath them, so that we would not emerge on the other side at the same point where we entered. It looked like a crash-up derby, the way the trucks in our convoy slipped left and right across all three lanes at each overpass.

After a while, traffic became very heavy. All three lanes were blocked with traffic, so we pulled onto the median and drove past all of them, kicking up our own cloud of dust, and pulling back on about a hundred meters later. The MSR was packed with military convoys in both directions. Old units were driving south to Kuwait, and the new units were heading north into Iraq. Huge trucks hauling shipping containers and a variety of armored vehicles lined the freeway by the hundreds for several miles. There were artillery ammo carriers loaded on trucks, which I found odd, as there really wasn't anything left in Iraq to fire artillery at any more. Next came tracked engineer vehicles, followed by a heavy tracked maintenance unit with M-88 armored recovery vehicles. Even though the M-88s were resting on trailers and being pulled by trucks, each one had a Soldier in the commander's cupola manning the heavy machine gun, scanning the countryside as they headed north. These were all part of OIF 2.

We arrived at BIAP and checked into our tents for the night. Our C-130 was scheduled to leave the following afternoon. Then we would finally be out of Iraq.

DAY 285: FRI 12 MAR 04

Our take-off was at 1720, and we corkscrewed steeply into the sky over Baghdad in a vain attempt to avoid any last attempts to down us with missiles, before turning south towards Kuwait. While the possibility of the missile threat always loomed every time a plane took to the sky, it was relatively easy for me to put it out of my mind. After all, despite scores of C-130s criss-crossing all over Iraq on a daily basis, and despite the C-130's relatively large size and slow speed, not one had been shot down or even hit by a missile—to date. All I had to hope was that we would not be the first. The light began to dim through the small, round windows as the sun began to set.

It was over. After 285 days in Iraq, we were finally out. We spent the following days at Doha cleaning and packing equipment and attending briefings. The company's equipment had been cleaned, inspected and re-packed into the shipping containers. During that time, I ran into Fuwad, the linguist from Diwaniyah, on the streets of Camp Doha. His forehead was heavily scabbed, and had dozens of surgical stitches in two different places. His nose and hands were also scabbed.

Shocked, I asked him, "Fuwad, what happened to you?"

"I had been riding in a Humvee on the highway from Diwaniyah to Hilla when the driver, SPC Lopez, left the road and flipped the Humvee. She's in the hospital in a coma with a fractured neck and jaw. The other passenger, First Lieutenant Vega, is also in a coma. He's already been medevaced to Germany."

Lopez was a new Soldier from our battalion that had just completed her initial entry training and had been mobilized to backfill our replacement unit as part of OIF 2. She was later evacuated to Walter Reed for several months of rehabilitation. Unfortunately, Lieutenant Vega died several days later, never having awoken from his coma. Of the three, Fuwad was the lucky one.

A review of the situation reports revealed that the battalion staff had made four convoys from their headquarters at BIAP to a local school during the deployment, yet they had visited our company only twice in a ten-month period. Even more appalling, a majority of one company's soldiers were at Camp Slayer, a mere three miles away on the other side of the airfield. The command staff didn't even have to suit up in their body armor to go there. Yet, according to those Soldiers that were assigned there, *not even once* did the battalion leadership visit them to check in on their welfare, see how they were doing, or to lend an ear to any of their issues—all of which were the prime responsibilities of leaders. Many Soldiers believed that their leaders just lacked the courage to leave the confines of BIAP for fear of putting themselves at risk of being shot at or ambushed, even though their own Soldiers were living and working outside the wire every day.

Battalion logistical support throughout the entire deployment had been appallingly dismal. The battalion headquarters had tried to *take* our company's water buffalo while they were trying to survive in the desert, instead of providing more support. Soldiers had been left stranded at BIAP with no food or water for days on end, having to beg from neighboring units like street vagrants. The battalion maintenance section had made only a *single* maintenance run to our company to repair deadlined vehicles during the entire yearlong deployment. The battalion had made only a single mail run to our company during the entire deployment—one of their primary responsibilities as leaders in caring for their Soldiers—and had even held our mail hostage at one point. The rest of the time, they required the company to run their own convoys to the battalion to get their own mail, something that companies never should have had to do. This of course put the companies continually at risk of ambush, while the headquarters personnel remained safely and comfortably inside their camp. Companies had been forced to beg to get their broken vehicles towed and repaired by other units. We never did receive the necessary communications equipment to perform our duties in the safe manner required by SOP. The Interceptor vests necessary to protect the Soldiers didn't arrive until December, and even then didn't have the right size of ceramic plate inserts to make them effective against AK-47 rounds. If it hadn't been for the vest loaned to me by the OGA in my *ninth* month in theater, I would have gone through the entire deployment without proper ballistic protection. The Soldiers had *never* received their authorized extra uniform issue. B Company had moved their shipping containers on their own to avoid having them getting lost or delayed by battalion, as what happened to C Company's. Then there had been the lack of coordination on turning in the tents. The battalion's logistical efforts had been a complete and unmitigated disaster from beginning to end.

We had armed ourselves with captured Iraqi weapons, drove in trucks loaned to us from the Marines, and used telephones and body armor borrowed from the OGA—all of which were necessities to fight the war, but none of which had been provided to us by our own Army. We were Soldiers for the wealthiest nation on Earth serving in a combat zone, but had to beg for ammo, which was always in short supply and very difficult if not impossible to obtain through our own supply channels. Other units always seemed to have plenty. In spite of all this, the battalion S-4 was awarded a Bronze Star Medal. The battalion had done next to nothing to support or otherwise ensure the success of the companies. In fact, it would have been more accurate to state that the companies accomplished their missions *in spite of* interference and lack of support from the battalion.

It was a shining example of the extraordinary adaptability of our Soldiers to overcome obstacles, no matter where they came from. Adaptability sometimes required breaking the rules. Since our colonists had been shooting at formation-marching Redcoats from behind trees, a native disinclination of our Soldiers to adhere rigidly to rules had saved our military many times throughout the history of American warfare. The risks of military adaptation had grown in direct proportion to the need for it, and it relished in the American Soldier's inbred abilities to improvise. It was by no accident that many considered our Special Forces to be our most adaptable military instrument—that's the way they were trained and expected to behave. Some things in war never change.

On Friday the 26th of March, Major General Kimmons, the Commanding General of the U.S. Army Intelligence and

Security Command at Fort Belvior, Virginia, addressed the battalion. Originally, we had been told that Colonel Jones, the commander of the 500th MI Brigade, wanted to address the battalion and thank us for all of the good work that we had done, but then it switched to the general, and we heard nothing further about the colonel. Perhaps Colonel Jones had heard that there was a significant number of Soldiers in our battalion that had very bad feelings toward him after the way he and his brigade had treated us before they had left the previous June, and he changed his mind. Jones' brigade actually took necessary equipment away from our battalion back to the States with them when they rotated back home, just prior to us going into Iraq—equipment that we would desperately need to accomplish our mission, but now would not have available to us. The excuse was that the 500th brigade never knew when they would need to deploy again, so took our equipment "just in case." A number of Soldiers were so incensed at him that they were prepared to tell the colonel off to his face, respect and protocol be damned.

General Kimmons was the commander of all U.S. Army intelligence assets worldwide, and he had come to Kuwait hoping to go to Baghdad to visit with the 500th MI Brigade. They were just arriving in Iraq as part of the OIF-2 rotation. However, General Kimmons couldn't get permission to enter Iraq. From historical experience, generals were restricted from visiting combat zones, as they had a tendency to muddle and otherwise interfere with the chain of command. So, to prevent such interference, generals not assigned to the theater were kept on a tight leash in combat zones. The general talked for about 10 minutes and thanked us for our contributions in Iraq over the last year, emphasizing that despite what we may see or hear on the news when we get back home, the nation was very grateful for our sacrifices, and especially the sacrifices of our families.

We spent the remaining days waiting for our flight back to

the States, watching movies, sleeping, reading, relaxing, and doing basically anything to keep us from being bored out of our skulls—"decompressing" in new Army parlance. I started to get homesick again, knowing that we were so close to being home, and there was little to do to keep us occupied to make it seem that the time was passing faster. The days dragged by and the passage of time kept pace with continental drift.

Finally, two weeks after arriving at Doha, the day arrived for us to leave. We packed up and had our customs inspection of our personal baggage to ensure that no one was trying to bring home any explosive devices or other illegal items. A Soldier from another unit several months prior had managed to smuggle a land mine all the way back to Fort Dix before it was discovered. We ended up with only one small switchblade being confiscated by the Air Force Security Police that were doubling as customs inspectors.

We boarded our plane, a Boeing 757, at about nine the following morning and flew to Naples, Italy, then to Keflavik, Iceland, and from there to McGuire Air Force Base, New Jersey, arriving at about ten that same night. With the time zone changes, it had been a 32-hour day. About 16 of those hours had been spent stuffed inside the 757. But we were finally back in the USA, and that's all that mattered to us. The battalion had been deployed a total of 369 days.

During medical out-processing, several Soldiers received more Anthrax vaccinations per Army policy—even though we were going home, not into a combat zone to face possible biological contamination. It was a waste of resources, absurd on the face of it, and even more so since there had not been any discoveries of Anthrax in Iraq. When I told the civilian technician that there *was no* Anthrax threat, and asked him why we were getting the unnecessary vaccinations, he replied absurdly, "Anthrax is everywhere. It's in the grass in your front yard."

While waiting in the finance out-processing line, Major Baker was teasing one of my Soldiers. When I told the Soldier that the major was good at being a nuisance, Baker told me, "What are you talking about? I never bothered you that much."

"You did plenty, major," I replied sternly.

"What are you talking about? What did I do?"

"I had heard that you were the one that gave the order to take away all of the Iraqi weapons from our company. Is that true?"

"Yes."

"And you were aware that you left some of my Soldiers armed with only pistols to defend themselves in a combat zone against insurgents with AKs and RPGs?"

"Yes."

"Then I hold you responsible for putting me and my Soldiers in *greater* danger, and to me, that's unforgivable. I want you to know, major, that if one of my Soldiers had been killed or wounded in an ambush, I would have filed criminal charges against you."

The next day, he had the nerve to nonchalantly plop down next to me on the post shuttle bus as I was returning from lunch. "Going back to the hooch, chief?"

Again, I looked at him sternly and shook my head, "You just don't get it, do you." He just smiled at me with that idiotic-looking grin of his.

"Excuse me," I said. He got up, and I moved to another seat. I couldn't stand being near him. He came to represent everything that I had despised about the selfish incompetence of the field-grade MI officers that I had encountered seemingly throughout my tour of duty in Iraq.

Finally, the big day had arrived. The morning of the 5th of April was bitterly cold. Icicles had formed along the gutters of the roof, and the wind bit into any exposed flesh. The battalion huddled in the foyer as we waited for the buses to arrive to take us home.

Eventually, the buses showed up. We convoyed southward,

noting the number of yellow ribbons that lined the roads leading into the post. We parked and off-loaded in front of the post recreation center. The building entrance was filled with families, all shouting and screaming as we off-loaded and stacked our bags.

The entire battalion formed up and marched single file into the meeting hall, while a military band played in the far corner. We all stood at parade rest in the middle of the room, surrounded on all sides by family and press. The hall was lined with yellow ribbons, posters and "welcome home" banners.

A number of dignitaries gave unmemorable but short speeches, to include the post commander, the commanding general of the regional readiness command, and the battalion commander. Then came the order, "Battalion, dismissed!" The families let out a howl, and charged into our dissembling formation to meet their loved ones. Television crews and reporters were not far behind, filming the reunions for the evening news, and interviewing various Soldiers. Within an hour, the hall was empty. Our liberation was finally complete.

EPILOGUE

On March 28th, Bremer ordered Sadr's newspaper, *Al-Hawza al-Natiqah* (The Outspoken Hawzah), closed down for inciting violence against the U.S. occupation. The newspaper was widely perceived as Sadr's mouthpiece; the CPA rightfully accused it of printing lies that stirred up anti-U.S. sentiment.

During his "sermon" at the Kufa mosque on Friday, April 2nd, Sadr sounded a call to arms, and declared his allegiance with two major anti-Western Islamic fundamentalist terrorist organizations, the *Hamas* and the *Hizballah,* both supported by the Iranian regime. Then, the Coalition arrested one of his junior clerics in Sadr City in Baghdad for spreading anti-Coalition rhetoric. Simultaneously, some of Sadr's militia surreptitiously infiltrated the Ali shrine for Friday prayers. They then told the shrine's keeper, Mr. Killidar, that they had no shelter, and asked to spend the night within the complex, as is customary for traveling pilgrims.

On Saturday, April 3rd, Sadr's infiltrators brought out guns and forced out all of the shrine employees, effectively taking control of the shrine. Sadr finally controlled the symbol of his power that he had longed for. He then took possession of the donations in the shrine's vault. In the six months before Sadr had taken control of the shrine, it had collected over a half million dollars in Iraqi currency in donations from pilgrims, as well as untold amounts of contributions in Iranian, Syrian and Lebanese currencies. This booty now became Sadr's new war chest.

Bremer ordered the arrest of Sadr's senior aide, Mustafa al-Yaqubi, in Najaf, who was wanted along with Sadr for the killing of rival cleric Ayatollah al-Khoei the previous April.

That evening, using a dinner invitation as bait, Lieutenant Colonel Sayeed, the Kufa chief of police, and his deputy, Major Kassem were lured into an ambush and killed by assassins firing AKs at point blank range into his car in a narrow alley. My team members and I had visited with both of them on numerous occasions, and had known them personally. Their murders had been ordered by Sadr personally in preparation for his uprising against the Coalition that began the following day, as he felt that as a key figure, Sayeed was too charismatic, and could possibly rally his police officers in opposition against him.

The next morning, Sunday, April 4th, 17 Salvadoran soldiers from the *Cuscatlan* airborne commando Battalion drove in their five-ton truck to the low-walled Iraqi Civil Defense Corps (ICDC) camp about 1.2 miles from Camp Baker for a shift of jail guard duty, which they pulled jointly with some of the newly-trained Iraqi soldiers. This was the same camp that had been originally built by Saddam to train the Jerusalem Liberation Army, and U.S. Navy Seabees had recently built a small jail there to handle the overcrowding from the local jails around the city. The parade grounds were used to train one of the first new battalions of the ICDC.

There were supposed to be about 350 ICDC soldiers in the camp, but the Salvadorans were a bit surprised to find it largely deserted upon their arrival. The Iraqi soldiers had gotten the word that something was going to happen, and that in the interests of their own future health, they should not bother showing up to work that morning.

Shortly thereafter, the small group of Salvadoran soldiers found themselves surrounded and trapped by a large contingent of heavily-armed *Mahdi* Army thugs, who opened up on them and began besieging the base with rifle, machine gun and RPG fire.

Back at the main base of Camp Baker, about 700 *Mahdi* Army opened fire and attempted to overrun the camp. A four-hour gun battle ensued. *Mahdi* members seized control of the adjacent hospital, the tallest building in the city, which provided a dangerous vantage point overlooking all of Camp Baker. The ranking American officer on location was the signal platoon leader, a young lieutenant. Fortunately, being a signal officer, he had the most powerful weapon in the American arsenal at his disposal: the radio. The lieutenant called for Apache helicopters and close air support. His requests for Medevac for his wounded Soldiers were disapproved, as the area was declared too hot. He was heard screaming into his mike, "The *Mahdi* Army are crossing the wire, and the f---ing Spanish aren't doing anything!!!"

The Salvadorans and U.S. Soldiers from the signal detachment, and eight mercenaries from Blackwater Security tried to protect the camp perimeter and retake the hospital. Shockingly, even with their own base under attack, the Spanish soldiers actually *refused to fight*, and only after a long delay finally agreed to send out their armored cars to help evacuate the wounded Salvadorans from the nearby ICDC camp.

Fearful of inflicting civilian casualties, the Salvadorans at the ICDC camp took cover and, demonstrating a high level of combat discipline, *held their fire* for nearly half an hour, as one by one they became wounded from enemy fire. Once ten of them were wounded, they figured that they had held back long enough, and only then began returning fire in an effort to defend themselves. After several hours, they were out of ammo. Each soldier had brought a standard basic load of only 300 rounds with them. Private Natividad Mendez lay dead, riddled by two bullets probably fired by a sniper. Two more were wounded as the close-quarters fighting intensified.

The four remaining uninjured soldiers struggled to load the wounded back onto the truck to try to make a run for the hospital when they were attacked and swarmed by ten *Mahdi* thugs who attempted to take one of them hostage. It was at that point that Corporal Samuel Toloza said a prayer, whipped out his switchblade knife and charged the Iraqi gunmen.

In one of the few known instances of hand-to-hand combat in the Iraq conflict to that date, Toloza stabbed several attackers who were swarming around one of his comrades as they attempted to drag him away as a hostage. The stunned assailants backed away momentarily, just as a relief column from Camp Baker came to their rescue.

"We never considered surrender. I was trained to fight until the end," said Toloza.

General Sanchez flew on a Blackhawk helicopter to Camp Babylon that morning to confer with the Polish division commander on what became the opening volleys in the First Battle of Najaf. Ukrainian units were sent in as a Quick Reaction Force to break the siege on Camp Baker, and break out the Coalition forces trapped there.

By the end of the day, four Salvadoran soldiers were killed, and an estimated 300 *Mahdi* Army terrorists had been killed. The blood letting had begun. The *Mahdi* Army now occupied the Ali shrine itself, the real prize of the city that Sadr had been trying to gain control of for all these months. Whoever controlled the shrine controlled Najaf itself, as the shrine was the heart, soul and body of Najaf.

They had also taken control of the government buildings and police stations all across southern Iraq, in an unmistakably direct challenge to Coalition authority. Some of the very policemen that we had worked with on a daily basis had now joined the *Mahdi* Army after the police stations were occupied.

I was relieved not to have been a part of it, and that my team was now home.

But it had been a close call. Shortly after our battalion had packed away all of our weapons and equipment, and were waiting at Camp Doha, Kuwait, to fly back to the States, General Sanchez requested that our battalion be *sent back into Iraq* for an additional 90 days in light of the new violence. The only thing that had saved us from the involuntary extension was the fact that our weapons and equipment had already left for the port, and that we had no vehicles. If the request had come only a few days later, we could have found ourselves back in Najaf, and certainly mixed up in the middle of it all. 20,000 other U.S. Soldiers from the 1st Armored Division and the 2nd Armored Cavalry Regiment were not as fortunate, and did get extended for another three months. Those Soldiers could have gone home at the same time as us, if Sanchez had just listened to our reports about Sadr, in addition to the numerous staff officers that concurred with them, and taken appropriate, timely action. One bit of solace that those Soldiers received was an extra $1,000 per month until they did go home.

On April 7th, former Iranian president Akbar Hashemi Rafsanjani praised Sadr's actions as "heroic" during his Friday prayer sermon in Tehran. "Contrary to these terrorist groups in Iraq," referring to the Coalition, "there are powerful bodies which contribute to the security of that nation... among them is the *Mahdi* Army, made up of enthusiastic, heroic young people."

An April 11th report in London's Arabic newspaper *Al Sharq al-Awsat* claimed that the decision to activate the "*Shi'ite* resistance" had been made during a secret conference titled "Islamic Movement in Iraq" in Mid-March. The conference had been held in London, and had been attended by representatives of a number of unnamed major Islamic movements—including Sadr representatives and a representative from the prominent terrorist group *Hizballah*. Rumors also began to circulate that Sadr was seeking political asylum in Iran, and had sent representatives to meet with agents from the Iranian Intelligence Service to discuss how to smuggle Sadr out of Iraq.

Sadr enjoyed a close relationship with the terrorist *Mullahs* of Iran, the same ones that routinely tortured and murdered thousands of their own people in order to maintain their own power in the name of Islam, and support international terrorist groups like *Hizb-Allah*. We had reported a number of his trips to Iran to confer with Iranian officials during our tenure. Apparently, crossing the International Border between Iran and Iraq was fairly easy, despite Coalition efforts to the contrary.

On April 13th, Sistani attempted to call for restraint and reason on both sides, but his pleas fell on deaf ears. Two days later, Sistani added to the confusion when he declared the holy city of Najaf off limits to U.S. forces. That same day, Iranian diplomats traveled to Najaf to meet with Sadr. The following day, Khalil Naimi, an Iranian official, was assassinated in Baghdad. It was never discovered if there had been a correlation between these events.

The Spanish military commander in Iraq had refused to obey an order from General Sanchez to launch an offensive against the *Mahdi* Army in Najaf. Meanwhile, Jose Bono, the Spanish defense minister, said Spanish troops would *not* follow a U.S. order to hand over Sadr "dead or alive". The Spanish military command in the region blamed the month-old uprising on the incorrect reading of the situation by the Pentagon. In this case, the Spanish were right.

Since the election of a new Socialist prime minister three days after terrorist bombings on four Spanish trains killed 191 people, Jose Luis Rodriguez Zapatero, the people of Spain blindly caved into the pressure of international terrorism and elected a candidate that vowed to implement a Viet Nam-like withdrawal of its forces out of Iraq, giving Usama bin Laden exactly what he wanted: western withdrawal and nonparticipation in establishing freedom for Islamic-dominated people. Unfortunately, terrorists around the world were now emboldened to believe that their terrorist actions could influence national politics and policies, and would surely plan to act against other nations.

A force of British Royal Marines and an armored infantry battle group were mobilized in England and sent to Najaf to fill the security vacuum left by Spanish troops. Once again, our loyal British friends upheld their vow to support the Global War on Terror.

Spanish Army General Jose Enrique de Ayala told Spanish reporters in Diwaniya that he had disagreed with the U.S. strategy to "antagonize" the Iraqis loyal to Sadr, who the Spanish Army had allowed to take control of Najaf. He said the contingent of 200 Spanish soldiers was not prepared for the large-scale offensive action the U.S. demanded and it would have been contrary to Spain's mandate in Iraq. In a report to his superior, Polish General Mieczyslaw Bienek, General Ayala said: "We are not an offensive force. Our mandate was not that. Our mission was to contribute to the stabilization and reconstruction of Iraq. Moreover, we do not have the means to develop a strategic offensive."

During the uprising, the Spanish troops limited their operations to defending their base, which came under attack by the *Mahdi* Army. They refused to leave their base and go into the city to protect the citizens and re-establish order, as was their responsibility.

A brigade of U.S. troops from the 1st Armored Division had to move into Najaf in mid-March to re-establish order. The U.S. forces closed the *Al-Hawza Nataq* newspaper, which Sadr supported, and arrested his lieutenant, Mustafa Yaquibi, which had sparked the violent uprising. General Ayala stated that had he been consulted, he would have advised against the arrest.

Contrary to General Ayala's opinion, the Coalition was not antagonizing Sadr; it was clearly the other way around.

The Spanish army had deployed an entire brigade to Iraq, which contained 1,300 soldiers, not just the 200 the colonel mentioned, and also had attached to them an infantry battalion each from Honduras and El Salvador. They had more than enough soldiers to establish order; they just refused to do it. Further, there was no requirement or necessity for anything resembling a "large-scale offensive," especially against a band of rag-tag street thugs with no military training or discipline who earlier would have scattered like cockroaches under a bright light at the first sound of gunfire. Our own lack of resolve to do anything about them when they blatantly displayed their weapons in public and we did nothing about it only increased their resolve. And it was *not* contrary to their mandate: it *was* their mandate to establish and maintain order, and they had utterly failed to do so. General Ayala just didn't want to handle the situation, resulting in the debacle that was now taking place.

When the Spanish troops started coming home from Iraq in early May 2004, the elation of their return had given way to a discontented silence among the soldiers who felt they had let down their allies. The Spanish soldiers expressed regret over leaving Iraq so hastily, and disappointment over a lack of official recognition on their return and the public's seeming willingness to forget them and their mission. Even soldiers that had disagreed with Spanish involvement from the outset felt that it was wrong to pull out.

The May 8, 2004, issue of the Iraqi daily *Al-Sabah*, reported that Zapatero had reached a secret agreement through an "Iraqi intermediary" with Sadr for protection of Spanish troops and personnel during their retreat from Iraq. The "Spanish end of the deal" remained unclear. What had Madrid agreed to in order to bring about the truce with Sadr's *Mahdi* Army?

Regardless of what the Spanish Government had or had not promised Sadr, the fact that Prime Minister Zapatero had reached an accord of any kind was significant in itself. It evidenced an increasingly clear pattern of European governments apparently demonstrating a willingness to reach separate agreements with militant Islamist elements in order to secure the perceived protection of their forces from attack. In essence, they were fraternizing with the enemy.

The retreat of Spanish forces from Iraq, following the March 11, 2004, Madrid bombings — especially within the context of a secret agreement with Sadr — was a significant strategic victory for the Tehran-Damascus-*al-Qaeda* axis.

Two days later, Poland and Bulgaria stressed their commitment to keep troops in Iraq "until we've done our job." Poland led the MND in south-central Iraq that included a Bulgarian contingent. Poland had 2,400 troops serving in Iraq, while Bulgaria had deployed 450 troops.

It justified everything that THT 108 had been pushing for during our time in Najaf. We had warned the Coalition repeatedly over the months that Sadr had been a threat to the Coalition and to stability in general, and that drastic action needed to be taken against him now rather than later. The longer Sadr was given to snub the Coalition, the more powerful and brazen he would become, until eventually he would challenge the Coalition in open warfare. That was our prediction, and because we had been ignored, that was what had now happened. And now people were dead on both sides. The people of Najaf had fallen victim to our own complacency. THT 108 had done their job, but our best efforts to draw attention to the problem had been ignored. CJTF-7 had accused us of biased reporting against Sadr, constantly urging them to take action to get rid of him earlier to avoid trouble later. Who was biased now? When did Mr. Bremer get this revelation that Sadr was an outlaw? We had been trying to pound that into the Coalition for the last eight months.

Months later, I talked with a friend of mine, a senior Military Intelligence sergeant, who had worked in the intelligence section of our brigade headquarters, and had read many of our reports insisting that Sadr be arrested before the situation got worse. He had taken them to his boss and insisted that the best way to handle it before the situation got out of hand was to declare martial law, a standard historical method for re-establishing order in an area after armed conflict and unrest. As he put it, "I don't even remember how many times I recommended the application of martial law, but I was always given the same answer: 'We are Americans, and we don't do things like that.'" Apparently, these officers were completely unfamiliar with history. Germany was under martial law and military administration for four years after World War II, and Japan for *seven* years.

Our work and subsequent recommendations to CJTF-7 were further justified by comments made by Major General Martin Dempsey, commander of the 1st Armored Division, who had a brigade surrounding Najaf to contain Sadr and the *Mahdi* Army. At a media briefing on May 11, 2004, Dempsey acknowledged that U.S. forces should have moved more quickly to detain or arrest Sadr last year, before he consolidated his militia. "Why didn't we marginalize him sooner?" Dempsey asked.

"Because in the course of the year that I've been here, and in the course of seeking advice from as many possible people as we could -- religious leaders, political leaders, tribal leaders -- as you might expect, we received such a wide variety of advice on how to deal with Muqtada al-Sadr that it caused us to be a little bit careful. He was training troops, gaining resources and stockpiling weapons," Dempsey said. "We probably gave him six months more than he should have had."

On May 11, 2004, about 400 people joined a peaceful demonstration in Najaf, demanding that the *Mahdi* Army leave the city. Many Najaf residents opposed Sadr's presence in the city because it had paralyzed pilgrim tourism, which, other than the cemetery, was the mainstay of the city's economy.

Many of the locals believed that Sadr was deliberately destabilizing Iraq—on orders from Iran.

The primary fighting in Najaf took place during May 14-24 in the cemetery. There were nightly battles against an estimated 2,500 fighters. Initially, General Sanchez had declared the cemetery an exclusion zone, meaning that Soldiers could not enter, and could only fire at identified targets. This only served to provide a sanctuary for the enemy. The enemy fired a total of 495 mortar rounds from inside the Kufa mosque.

American Soldiers sent in to fight the *Mahdi* Army stated that they were winning, and that the militia was very surprised, because they were not used to having people fire back at them and pursue them. That was because the Spanish army never did. The militiamen had set up mortar positions inside the cemetery. The fighters also had pills, believed to be valium. Americans said they didn't think much of the rebel tactics, describing it as more like a street-gang kind of fight. As we had always stated, the *Mahdi* Army were not professionals that we needed to worry about.

On Saturday, May, 22, 2004, members of the Iraqi Counterterrorism Force entered and cleared the green-domed Salah Mosque across the street from the Kufa police station, seizing a .30-caliber machine gun, two 60-millimeter mortar tubes, 12 rocket-propelled grenades, more than 200 82-millimeter mortar rounds and rocket-propelled grenade launchers. The Iraqi commandos had been trained at Camp Babylon by Special Forces specifically for use on mosque raids.

The American military was justified in attacking mosques and shrines because insurgents used such buildings as arsenals. Doing so nullified their protected status under the Geneva Conventions as religious sites, and made them legitimate military targets. The assaults did not result in large protests in Iraq, which was an indication of how unpopular Sadr was in the southern towns he had seized. A cleric in Najaf said: "When Saddam was ousted we were happy. But the Americans have made many, many mistakes. They haven't respected any of our traditions or Islamic values. Al-Sistani believes in getting rid of the Americans using peaceful methods. Muqtada al-Sadr believes in violence. The methods are different but the goals are the same. We are all united in this aim."

In effect, Sadr's revolt was not only anti-American, but anti-establishment. He upset the traditional *Shi'ite* religious hierarchy, where influence rests with a few aged wise men. In *Shi'ite* terminology, Sistani represents the "silent seminary" that shies from speaking out directly on social or political issues, and focuses on religious issues. Sadr came to represent the "speaking seminary," which wasn't shy at all about tackling political issues head-on, as he proved in April of 2004.

Sadr and his followers also took the opportunity during their uprising to eliminate anyone in Najaf that had any connections to the former *Ba'athists*. It was open season on those who had worked for or associated with Saddam's party. Hundreds were killed.

A cease-fire was declared on June 4th. Since the fighting had begun almost two months prior on April 8th, 19 American Soldiers had been killed, and an estimated 1,500 terrorists. The 1st Armored Division had liberated Al Kut, Diwaniya, Karbala, Kufa and Najaf.

On June 28, 2004, Bremer formed the new Iraqi government and handed it over to the Iraqis. He had moved the hand-over up by two days from the previously-scheduled end of the month in order to thwart any planned terrorist attacks against the new government on that day. It also made Bremer look like he couldn't wait to pass the buck and get the hell out of Dodge before the situation got any worse.

In July, 2004, Iraq's interim Prime Minister, Ayad Allawi, in a clear rejection of Bremer's approach, issued a decree allowing Sadr to re-open the *Al Hawza* newspaper. In mid-July, the *Mahdi* Army began regrouping with help from Iranian intelligence agents. The militia was storing weapons in two so-called unpatrolled "exclusion zones," the vast cemetery, and the Imam Ali Shrine. Some 80 Iranian intelligence agents were working with an estimated 500 *Mahdi* militiamen, providing training and nine 57-millimeter Russian-made antiaircraft guns, in addition to stockpiles of antitank weapons, mortars, and other armaments. The thugs also continued to terrorize the local population, kidnapping police officials and their family members, arbitrarily "arresting" citizens, and occupying buildings in Najaf.

The tension exploded again on August 4th, when Marines newly assigned to Najaf were ambushed while patrolling the city streets. Sadr's spokesman announced that the Marines initiated the trouble by violating the previously-established "exclusion zones," by driving past one of Sadr's residences.

On August 7th, Iraqi police in Karbala deported about 1,000 Iranian citizens. The following day, they arrested 28 Iranians and three Afghans.

On August 9th, Iraqi Prime Minister Iyad Allawi demanded that the *Mahdi* Army withdraw from Najaf or face removal by force. The governor of Najaf, Adnan al-Zurufi, said, "There is Iranian support for Sadr's group, and this is no secret. We have information and evidence that they are supplying the *Mahdi* Army with weapons and have found such weapons in their possession." There were also reports of Former Regime Loyalists fighting alongside the *Mahdi* Army, and providing combat instruction to the militia members in the use and employment of mortars and RPGs inside the Kufa mosque. Additional weapons were smuggled into the Kufa mosque in trucks under loads of watermelons. Iraqi police searched the vast cemetery for a group of 80 Iranian fighters that was reportedly holed up there.

With the tenuous approval of the interim Iraqi government, the Coalition wasted no time in assembling forces, and on August 12th, kicked off a second offensive against the *Mahdi* Army.

At midnight on August 25th, U.S. Marine and Army units stormed into the old city to gain a foothold and pave the way for the final assault into the shrine. The 4th Marines moved south through the center of the cemetery to the road circling the old city, then moved counter-clockwise until they were on the west end. Then they swung back east and fought towards the shrine. Two Army battalions launched a simultaneous assault from the east end, forming a pincer on the shrine itself and pressuring the terrorists from both sides. Once the shrine was surrounded, two Iraqi battalions totaling 1,400 soldiers followed that Marines from the west and took the shrine. At the start of the attack, it was estimated that the terrorists numbered about 3,000.

After 30 hours of continuous house-to-house fighting, Sadr realized that his *Mahdi* Army was being annihilated, and that his gig was up. On August 27th, he agreed to a political deal brokered by Grand Ayatollah Sistani, who had returned from heart surgery in Britain, to end the fighting. As the U.S. forces were within arms reach of the shrine, another cease-fire was called. Sistani's true motive was to save the shrine from destruction. With the *Mahdi* Army crippled, the Coalition leadership falsely believed that Sadr was no longer a threat, and as part of the cease-fire, allowed the grand terrorist Sadr to go free.

Soldiers and Marines fighting the *Mahdi* Army found evidence of drug use during both the April and August uprisings in Najaf. The conduct of many of the insurgents during the fighting suggested that they had ingested drugs that enabled them to continue fighting even after being severely wounded. Some described it as like watching the *Night of the Living Dead*, as people who should have been dead were still alive. At one point, a Marine machine gunner put five rounds into one terrorist who just stood there and took it, and then took off running. Marines changed their strategy and focused on head shots, because body shots were apparently not good enough. Numerous locations with stockpiles of syringes were found in the terrorist stronghold areas after the battles. After the battles, ironically it was the surviving terrorists that told that they had proudly protected the shrines from the evil drug-selling Americans.

During the cease-fire in August, the Coalition paid Sadr $1.2 million buying back weapons from his *Mahdi* Army. Another $330 million in reconstruction funds were made available to re-build the destruction done to Najaf. Undoubtedly, Sadr made good use of the American taxpayers' money to front his representatives in the new Iraqi government. His influence ran broad and deep, especially in the Ministry of Interior, which was responsible for the nation's police forces.

The Washington Times finally reported on September 1st that Sadr's thugs had been using a secret Muslim court to convict, torture and murder the radical cleric's opponents. The interim Iraqi government invited Sadr to join the political process and participate in the national elections that were held in January 2005. But how do you let into politics a *Shi'ite* leader whose army murders and mutilates innocents? In the Middle East, it's no big deal, just business as usual.

On September 19th, officials from both the State Department and the Pentagon described intelligence reports to the public that money, weapons and "a small number of" fighters were flowing across the border from Iran and assisting Sadr's forces. The officials stated that the monetary support was especially critical in keeping his movement alive, as it allowed Sadr to hire additional fighters and purchase more weapons. The hiring of fighters from outside areas, and even other countries, was vital, since Sadr was not popular among the local business class and moderates in and around Karbala and Najaf, especially since the battles destroyed their homes and businesses.

Explosive Ordnance Disposal teams found 367 roadside bombs in the cemetery and the streets around the shrine during and after the battle. One bomb weighing 3,000 pounds was found at a key intersection. 18,000 rounds of heavy-caliber machine-gun ammunition had been stockpiled, along with 28 tons of munitions inside the parking garage across the street from the shrine.

Sadr's arsenal had been no fly-by-night operation, but clearly had external support. The Najaf standoff had been created by Iran. It was only part of Iran's latest effort to destabilize Iraq and achieve strategic dominance in the Middle East and Central Asia. In Iraq, Iran aims to replicate its successes in Lebanon. Since Iraq's liberation, Iran has been providing weapons, money, and personnel to the *Mahdi* Army with the apparent goal of establishing an Iraqi version of *Hizb-Allah*, that, in time, would establish de-facto Iranian control over *Shi'a* Iraq. Despite his setback in Najaf, Sadr almost certainly will continue to do his masters' bidding.

Once the second battle ended, whoever survived from the Sadrist elements disbanded and returned home. Many of them began telling stories of a climactic struggle between good and evil, and outlandish tales of divine intervention. There were the "great birds" that came in and supposedly deflected American bombs from destroying the Ali shrine, which was never targeted despite its illegal use as a military stronghold. Then there were the tales of angels disabling American tanks.

The stories that were not told by anyone, including our own media, were the kidnapping of Iraqi police officers, city council members, and anyone else suspected of supporting the Coalition or the new government, their trials in Sadr's secret kangaroo courts, followed by their eventual brutal torture and "execution" for their so-called crimes. Then there were the 200-plus headless bodies of innocent Iraqi men, women and children discovered *inside* the "holy" shrine. There was even a body found that had been stuck into a bread oven and baked. Then there were the huge stockpiles of weapons and ammunition stacked high everywhere inside the shrine.

The Customs Police were one of the few entities which

went relatively unharmed during the two battles for Najaf. Because General Hussein and three-fourths of his department were of the same tribe, which was also one of the largest *Shi'ite* tribes, they were able to stand their ground and not be challenged for control of their station, weapons, or vehicles. Though several of the customs officers were kidnapped by militia, it was done en route to work or on the way home.

The Customs Police had needed weapons, and in the end, they had become one of the best armed stations in the city. This was because they fought side-by-side with the coalition forces in the cemetery and were, through their questionable loyalties, able to capture or otherwise secure a number of heavy weapons from the battle field at the end of each of the two battles, to include heavy anti-aircraft guns. They were also given many vehicles, of which none were stolen or damaged. This was a bit unusual, as all of the other police stations in Najaf were over-run and looted. The equipment was put to good use in aiding them in patrolling the critical Saudi border, which leaked like a sieve.

It was no surprise that the Customs Police were corrupt and on the take—it is a way of life and part of the culture in the Middle East. Too much was still getting through on their watch. Toward the end of our follow-on team's deployment, they were able to connect General Hussein and his tribe to smuggling operations that dated back to the Saddam era. Keep in mind that he was one of the few police commanders who remained in office after the fall. It was a tribal tradition of smuggling.

Our follow-on THT made use of many of our reports as historical documentation that was used to drive missions for the 2nd Armored Cavalry Regiment and the Marines during the first and second battles for Najaf. It was reassuring to know that the hundreds of reports that we had prepared and submitted had finally been put to good use, albeit a bit too late to make the difference that we had hoped for.

During the uprisings, the *Mahdi* Army had used the large multi-level parking garage next to the Imam Ali shrine as their main command post. Much to the dismay of the locals, who took great offense for being pushed out by a bunch of rabble from different cities, and even other countries, the *Mahdi* Army had taken complete control of the old city around the shrine. Before surrendering the shrine itself, they had plundered it of all of its historical artifacts.

After both battles were over, a special section of the cemetery was set aside for the bodies of those that had been killed fighting against the infidel Americans. It was decorated with numerous green banners and plastered with dozens of posters of Sadr. After the battles, bodies flowed into the necropolis at about 125 per day, almost double the number prior to then. In fact, *Shi'ites* have been dying at such an astonishing rate, that the boundaries of the cemetery were expanded by an additional two square miles.

I learned later that there had been an operation completely in place to arrest or kill Sadr, in the summer of 2003. Unfortunately, it had been unintentionally timed to take place the same day as the establishment of the Iraqi Governing Council, on July 13. Bremer supposedly wanted to get rid of Sadr sooner and tried but failed to persuade Washington D.C. on at least three separate occasions, but Washington got cold feet every time, and authorization was never given. Seeking such authorization from pencil-neck bureaucrats on another continent when it should have been decided by the generals on the battlefield was micromanagement at its finest. Despite such claims by Bremer, he personally cancelled the July 13 operation at the last minute because he had felt that it would have been too politically sensitive to carry through with the operation on that day. He had also insisted that it be a zero-collateral damage operation, which flies in the face of military operations. These are the kinds of things that can happen when diplomats have authority over military operations. The blood of all the people killed by Sadr and his followers from that day in July 2003 to the present is on Bremer's hands.

Sadr's influence in Iraq was vast. He came close to establishing a state within a state, following the example of *Hizb-Allah* in Lebanon. The battles of Najaf in 2004 led to the premature collapse of Iraq's fledgling military forces. In 2005 and 2006, he expanded his territory, taking over the Interior Ministry, massively infiltrating the Iraqi police, and tasking the *Mahdi* Army to expel Sunnis from neighborhoods in Baghdad. He established more *Sharia* courts and executed large numbers of Iraqi citizens. The *Mahdi* Army established and ran their own traffic checkpoints, pushing out legitimate control of the Iraqi government. It took over gas stations and skimmed money to finance their operations.

But his own expansion also triggered his demise. As Sadr expanded his influence and his followers practiced their corruption and brutality, he also created resentment among much of the population. When General Petraeus took over the surge in 2007 and implemented his tried and tested counter-insurgency strategy, Sadr felt the pinch, and knew it was time to leave.

Ironically, the current Iraqi Prime Minister, Nouri Al-Maliki, owes his office to Sadr. The relationship between them is complex: Sadr's support initially helped to bring Maliki to power, while now Maliki finds himself in the position of ordering crackdowns against the *Mahdi* militia. Showing fresh political resolve against unauthorized militias, Maliki ordered an offensive against *Mahdi* forces in Basra on March 24, 2008. Intelligence indicated that many of the *Mahdi* rogue factions were being supported by Iran. In reply, Sadr threatened to call an end to the cease-fire that he had called previously in August 2007. A renewed war with the *Mahdi* militia would paralyze southern Iraq and most certainly tie up any hope of a reduction in U.S. forces.

In April 2007, Sadr retreated to Iran. After his admitted

failure to rid Iraq of the U.S. occupation or to turn it into an Islamic society like Iran, his new goal is to bolster is clerical credentials so that he can garner the respect of an Ayatollah like Sistani, and hopefully be in place to fill his power vacuum when he passes on. Sadr's chief spokesman, Sheik Salah Al-Obeidi, stated, "He remains actively involved in the political field and will return when the time is right." Given Sistani's advanced age, this may happen soon.

Sadr lives with his new Persian bride in a posh 14-bedroom villa facing the snow-capped Towchall mountains in Tehran's exclusive Farmanieh neighborhood. Twice a week, he rides in his bulletproof limousine under armed escort to the holy city of Qom. While it normally takes at least 12 years of intensive study to become a *mutjahid* (one who offers religious guidance), Sadr's Iranian groomers have him on a crash course that should have him completed in four-to-five years. After that, Iran could have someone write his dissertation for him, and then be indorsed by one of their own Ayatollahs. By 2012, Sadr may be awarded with his own title of Ayatollah, and in position to control Najaf. From there, he would be able to influence Iraq's *Shi'a* majority, and thus Iraq. With Sistani soon out of the picture, Sadr would be Iran's man in Iraq. Iran could then be in position to fulfill Ayatollah Khomeini's grand vision of "liberating Jerusalem via Karbala."